Johannes Kepler

and the New Astronomy

IOANNES KEPPLERVS S. CÆS. MAIEST. ET ORDD. SVP. AVSTRIÆ MATHEMATICVS. &c.

Argentina

Owen Gingerich
General Editor

Johannes Kepler

and the New Astronomy

James R. Voelkel

Oxford University Press
New York • Oxford

for Katy

Oxford University Press

Oxford   New York
Athens   Auckland   Bangkok   Bogotá   Buenos Aires   Calcutta
Cape Town   Chennai   Dar es Salaam   Delhi   Florence   Hong Kong
Istanbul   Karachi   Kuala Lumpur   Madrid   Melbourne   Mexico City
Mumbai   Nairobi   Paris   São Paulo   Singapore   Taipei   Tokyo
Toronto   Warsaw

and associated companies in

Berlin   Ibadan

Copyright © 1999 by James R. Voelkel
Published by Oxford University Press, Inc.
198 Madison Avenue, New York, New York 10016
www.oup-usa.org

Oxford is a registered trademark of Oxford University Press

Design: Design Oasis
Layout: Leonard Levitsky
Picture research: Lisa Kirchner

Library of Congress Cataloging-in-Publication Data
Voelkel, James R. (James Robert)
Johannes Kepler and the New Astronomy / James R. Voelkel
p. cm. -- (Oxford portraits in science)
Includes bibliographical references and index.
Summary: A biography of the German astronomer who discovered three
laws of planetary motion.
ISBN 0-19-511680-1 (hardcover); 0-19-515021-X (paperback)
1. Kepler, Johannes, 1571-1630 Juvenile literature. [1. Kepler, Johannes,
1571-1630. 2. Astronomers.] I. Title. II. Series.
QB36.K4V64 1999
520'.92--dc21   99-23844
[B]   CIP

9 8 7 6 5 4 3

Printed in the United States of America
on acid-free paper

On the cover: Portrait of Kepler by Hans von Aachen (1612). Scholars are not
entirely certain that this portrait depicts Kepler. *Inset:* Detail of the frontispiece of
the Rudolfine Tables showing Kepler at work.
Frontispiece: Copperplate engraving of Kepler (1620) by Jacob von Heyden, after
a portrait by an unknown artist.

Contents

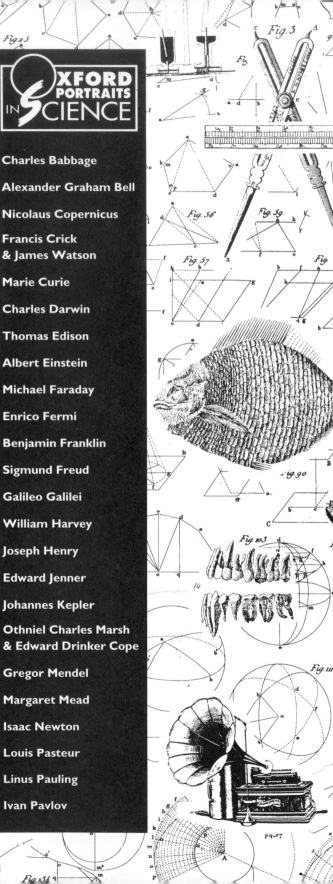

OXFORD PORTRAITS IN SCIENCE

"It can be said that among the men whose genius enriched and deep-ened human knowledge by creative achievements in the area of exact science there is hardly one who enjoys the sympathy of as many as does Kepler, despite the facts that his principal field of activity is unfa-miliar to most and that the result of his labors is difficult to understand and appreciate. It is the halo of his personality which draws many under his spell, the nobility of his character which makes friends for him, the vicissitudes of his life which arouse sympathy, and the secret of his union with nature that attracts all those who seek something in the universe beyond, and different from, that which rigorous science offers. In their hearts they all quietly bear veneration and love for this exceptional man. For no one who has once entered the magic sphere that surrounds him can ever escape from it."

—**Max Caspar,** *Kepler*

This contemporary woodcut depicts the Comet of 1577. The artist has included himself in the foreground, sketching the comet with the help of an assistant who holds a lantern.

The Comet

The year 1577 was graced with one of the most spectacular comets in recorded history. With a resplendent head that outshone any star and a tail 50 times the breadth of the full moon, it wheeled majestically through the heavens, exciting attention and comment throughout Europe. Deep in southern Germany in the duchy of Württemberg, Katharina Kepler led her five-year-old son Johannes up the hill overlooking the village of Leonberg to view the spectacle. His weak vision made more bleary by the late hour, the comet did not make much of an impression on him. But he would always remember his mother's kind gesture from an otherwise harsh and difficult childhood. At the same moment, far to the north on his private island in the Danish Sound, a young nobleman took time out from the task of building the world's greatest astronomical observatory to make detailed nightly observations of the comet.

Comets appear without warning in the heavens, which are otherwise the most regular and enduring feature of our environment. As such, at the time comets were viewed as fateful omens, signs that a change was in store. If the magnificence of the sign were any indication of its significance, this change would be very, very big. Perhaps it foretold the death of the emperor or of the sultan of the Turks, or maybe even the second coming of Christ was at hand. As it turned out, the comet did foretell a change, for along with the thousands of people who flocked out at night to gawk fearfully at the specter, here and there a handful of astronomers took careful, precise measurements that would eventually lead to a revolution in thought. The Scientific Revolution was dawning. And the little boy who stood yawning on the hill would be one of its most important thinkers.

Johannes Kepler was born on December 27, 1571, at 2:30 P.M. in his grandfather Sebald's small but commodious house in the city of Weil der Stadt. He was his parents' first child, and his father Heinrich was still living with his parents. The Keplers were a once proud and noble family, now in decline. Generations before, in 1433, Kepler's great-great-great-great-grandfather had been knighted by Emperor Sigismund in recognition of his valiant military service. Since then, in gradual steps, the family had left imperial service, fallen out of the nobility, entered the craftsman class, and moved to the small, sleepy city of Weil der Stadt. But the Keplers still cherished their former glory. They still had their family coat of arms, and tales were told of the military honors won by Kepler's great-grandfather and grandfather under Emperor Charles V and his successors.

Although not as illustrious as they had once been, the Kepler family had a respectable place in the life of Weil der Stadt. Grandfather Sebald, with his red, fleshy face, distinguished-looking beard, and fine clothes, was an authoritative man who had been mayor for ten years when Kepler was born. His election as mayor was a reflection of his high standing in the community, especially since the Keplers were members of the minority Protestant community there. As a leader, Sebald was more dictator than negotiator, but his advice was sound and the community trusted him. Still, he struck young Johannes as irascible and stubborn.

Sebald was the patriarch of the family and the closest thing Johannes would have to a father figure. The Kepler family's long slide seems to have reached bottom with Johannes's father Heinrich, Sebald's fourth son. He was a brutal, uneducated man who was absent for much of Kepler's childhood. Kepler wrote of his father, "He destroyed everything. He was a wrongdoer, abrupt, and quarrelsome." The martial spirit by which generations of Keplers had distinguished themselves in service to the emperor seems to have overflowed in Heinrich. Oppressed by the tight quarters of his father's house, Heinrich left before his son was three years old to seek adventure as a mercenary soldier fighting in Holland. This would be a pattern throughout Johannes's childhood. His father would return for a time, but the lure of the battlefield would call him back. When he was home, he was a hard and bad-tempered man. Finally, in 1588, when Kepler was sixteen, his father left, never to be seen again. It was rumored that he fought as a naval captain for the Kingdom of Naples and perished in Augsburg on his way home, but no one ever knew for sure.

Kepler was raised mostly by his mother, Katharina, the daughter of Melchior Guldenmann, who was the innkeeper and mayor of the village of Eltingen. Kepler took after her in many ways. Like her, he was small, wiry, and dark. They both possessed restless, inquisitive minds. Kepler's mother did not have formal schooling, but she was interested in the healing power of herbs and homemade potions, a pastime that would have very unfortunate consequences when she was an old woman and was put on trial as a suspected witch. There is no doubt that Katharina Kepler was also a strange, unpleasant woman whom people did not like. She too easily turned her sharp wit to the attack. Kepler himself described her as "sharp-tongued, quarrelsome, and possessing a bad spirit." The relationship between Kepler's brutal father and shrewish mother was certainly explosive, and it must have created an unbearable atmosphere in the home when Heinrich was not off soldiering somewhere. Years later, when Kepler used astrological principles to calculate the time of his conception, he arrived at the answer 4:37 in the morning on May 17, 1571. Since he had been a small and sickly baby, he disregarded the fact that his parents had only been married on May 15 and concluded he had been born prematurely, a "seven-months baby." If we view his conclusion with skepticism, the image of a hasty marriage precipitated by an unplanned pregnancy completes the picture of his parents' unhappy relationship.

Kepler was the first of seven children borne by his mother. Of these, only four grew to adulthood, a level of infant mortality not uncommon in the sixteenth century. Two years later, another son, Heinrich, was born. Like his namesake, he became a restless and unlucky man, whose life became a series of misadventures in which he was continually the victim of life-threatening accidents, beatings, and robberies. Kepler's other siblings were far less adventurous and led quite ordinary lives. His sister Margarethe grew up and married a clergyman. The youngest child, Christoph, later entered the craftsman class, as his forebears had done, and became a respectable tinsmith.

Despite its small size of 200 or so citizens and their families, Weil der Stadt was an imperial free city. It was a free city in the sense that, although surrounded by the duchy of Württemberg, it was an independent unit in the patchwork of duchies, principalities, bishoprics, and cities that made up the Holy Roman Empire of the German Nation. The Holy Roman Empire stretched across all of Germany and Austria and included Bohemia in the east (the Czech Republic today) and parts of France and Holland in the west. It was ruled by the Holy Roman Emperor Rudolf II from his seat in distant Prague in Bohemia. As an imperial free city, Weil der Stadt owed its allegiance only to the emperor and sent its own representative to the Imperial Diet, the occasional mass assembly of all of the powers of the empire. Weil der Stadt's status and history also meant that the practice of both Catholicism and Protestantism was allowed there, even though surrounding Württemberg was an aggressively Protestant state. The practice of religion in Germany at that time was an intensely disputed subject and one that would be of the utmost importance in Kepler's material, intellectual, and spiritual life.

The confessional struggles that would mark and mar Kepler's life had a history that was just over 50 years long at the time of his birth. After Martin Luther had broken with the Catholic church in 1517, proclaiming that faith alone justified man before God and that every person should read the Scriptures for himself, chaos had reigned for some time. The need for a reform of the Christian church—which was at that time almost exclusively Catholic in Western Europe—was deeply felt in the hearts of many people, especially in northern Europe. But political considerations clouded the picture as well. The Catholic church was a rich and powerful institution with its center of power located across the Alps in Rome. The prospect of seizing local assets from the Catholic church and evading its political power by joining with the Protestants appealed to many dukes and princes.

On the other hand, many felt a sincere loyalty to the Catholic church, which had upheld Christianity for more than a thousand years. Since Germany was not a unified country but a political patchwork, widespread religious and political upheaval engulfed the region. Finally, in an effort to restore order, an agreement was reached in the Religious Peace of Augsburg (1555), according to which each local leader would determine whether Catholicism or Protestantism would be practiced in his domain. The exception was the imperial free cities, like Weil der Stadt, in which both religions could continue to be practiced if they had previously done so. The situation in Weil der Stadt was further complicated by the fact that its urban area was entirely

Martin Luther broke with the Catholic church in 1517. The resulting religious upheaval had a strong effect on Kepler throughout his life.

surrounded by the duchy of Württemberg, whose duke was an important and powerful promoter of Protestantism. Thus, the Keplers found themselves in the unusual position of being members of a Protestant minority in a free city within a Protestant duchy.

Issues of religion played a powerful role in Kepler's education. Alone among his siblings, he was destined for a university education. By the time he set the first foot on this path at the age of five in 1577, his parents had moved the family from Weil der Stadt to the nearby town of Leonberg. Unlike the free city, Leonberg was part of the duchy of Württemberg, and so Kepler had access to the fine educational system the dukes had established for their subjects. He began in the ordinary German school, but was quickly moved to the Latin school, which was part of a parallel school system leading to the university. Whereas students in the German school learned the German they would need for their everyday life, students in the Latin school were taught to read and write in Latin, the international language of learning. Indeed, they were even required to speak only Latin to one another. Throughout Europe, serious study in any discipline was conducted in Latin, both in books and at universities, where even lectures and debates were in Latin. One strange result of Kepler's education was that, although his style in Latin was quite elegant, he never learned to write as well in his native language. He wrote all of his serious books and letters—even those to other Germans—in Latin.

A smooth ascent through the educational system was by no means assured for Kepler. He lost some time when the family moved again to Ellmendingen. Worse still, between 1580 and 1582, when he was eight to ten years old, he was set to hard agricultural labor by his parents. A small, weak child, he was unsuited to work in the fields, and it may have been a relief to parents and child alike to reenroll him in school. He gained a more serious foothold in the educational system when he passed state examinations and was admitted to the lower seminary at Adelberg on October 16, 1584. Lower seminary was the first of two steps leading to admission to the university. He did well and, two years later, proceeded to the higher seminary at the former Cistercian monastery at Maulbronn.

Perhaps because he was a small and sickly child or to escape from the unpleasant atmosphere of his childhood, Kepler delighted in difficult mental exercises, and he thrived in school. He became interested in poetry and meter and took pleasure in composing poems in difficult classical styles. Jokes and puzzles delighted him, and many of his poems employed tricks like anagrams (in which the letters can be rearranged to spell another word or phrase) and acrostics (in which the first letter of each line read downward forms a new word or phrase). To train his memory, he selected the longest Psalms to memorize.

Like his mother, he had a restless and inquisitive mind. As a result, his compositions would be full of digressions, as he leapt from one uncompleted thought to another. This quickness of mind and tendency to jump from one thought to another stayed with him throughout his life. And like his father, he expressed a certain amount of quarrelsomeness and violence. He was fiercely competitive. He made a list of his "enemies" from school (significantly, he left no list of friends), many of whom competed with him for high rankings in the class lists. When the lists were posted, spirits sometimes ran so high that fist fights broke out. Most of the time, a reconciliation was reached only when Kepler's rivals stopped challenging his academic supremacy.

Despite his occasional high spirits, Kepler was a serious and pious student. Even as a boy, he approached his religious studies with the greatest earnestness. He was never content simply to accept what he had been taught but always had to work it out for himself. So if he heard a sermon denouncing one Christian sect or another, he always made sure to follow the argument, compare it to what was actually said in the Bible, and come to his own conclusion. There were many subtle points of dogma that were erected as walls to separate the "true believers" from heretics, those who would not accept the standard teachings of the church. The ramparts of these walls were manned by serious young preachers who in their lessons and sermons fiercely denounced others' beliefs. Contentious disagreements existed not only with the Catholics but even more so between the various Protestant sects, chiefly the Lutherans and Calvinists. Most often Kepler saw the truth to lie somewhere between the positions staked out by the various sects, and he acknowledged that there was an element of truth even in "heretical" opinions. His willingness to concede the positive points of conflicting theological interpretations revealed his sincere faith and his good-hearted nature. His teachers tolerated his investigation of unorthodox and suspect beliefs because of his earnestness, but in his life he would learn that no amount of good faith and reasoned argument was sufficient to forge understanding between the Christian sects. Indeed, his efforts would end up alienating him from his own precious Lutheran community.

The culmination of Kepler's efforts in school came when Kepler passed the baccalaureate examination at the University of Tübingen on September 25, 1588. Even though he was still at the higher seminary at Maulbronn, he had officially been registered as a student at Tübingen for almost a year. He thus completed his undergraduate studies at Maulbronn and passed by examination at Tübingen, earning a B.A. degree without yet having attended classes there. The way was now open to proceed to the university to pursue an M.A. degree, and then to study at the university's seminary, where he would get advanced training in theology. After all these years of education, he would be able to enter service in the church, which had long become his greatest aspiration.

In early September of the following year, Duke Ludwig named five scholarship students to the *Stift*, the Lutheran seminary, at the University of Tübingen. Kepler was among them. By accepting the scholarship, Kepler was committing himself to lifelong service to the duke of Württemberg. In exchange, everything would be provided for him. The *Stift* would house and look after him while he completed two years of studies leading to his master's degree, and then take over responsibility for his additional three years of theological studies. He packed some personal possessions and set out for Tübingen. Around September 17, 1589, he signed his name in the registration book at the *Stift*:

> Johannes Kepler from Leonberg
> Born December 27, 1571

He was 17 years old. Following the normal course of study, Kepler would study two more years in the arts faculty of the university before devoting himself purely to theology. The two areas of his studies that interested him above the others and that remained his primary concerns for the rest of his life were mathematics (which included astronomy) and theology. The two subjects were alike in a way: both transcended our earthly experience in their quest for eternal truths. For Kepler, geometrical proofs seemed the closest we can come to certain knowledge in our mortal existence. And in astronomy, he saw in the layout of the solar system the image of God.

Kepler's teacher in mathematics and astronomy was Michael Maestlin, a solid and gruff-looking man whom Kepler admired deeply. The mathematical sciences were a specialty of Lutheran universities in Germany, and Maestlin was well qualified to teach Kepler the latest in astronomical theory: the heliocentric system of Nicolaus Copernicus, a Polish astronomer who had died 50 years earlier. In the heliocentric system, which means literally "sun-centered,"

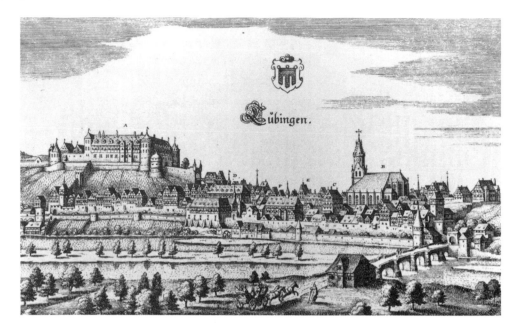

This engraving of Tübingen is by Matthäus Merian, who published a series of 16 books, the Topographia, that depicted many European towns and cities. Kepler attended the university in Tübingen.

the sun is at rest in the center of the solar system and the planets travel around it. Maestlin was quite unusual in actually believing this heliocentric system to be true. But he still taught the older geocentric (earth-centered) Ptolemaic astronomy to his beginning students.

Ptolemaic astronomy had been the dominant cosmological system, or view of the universe, for 1,500 years since its development by Claudius Ptolemy in the second century A.D. Ptolemy began with the knowledge—ancient even in his time—that the world is a sphere. In addition, he adopted the universal belief that it was at rest in the center of the universe, which was bounded on the outside by the sphere of stars. To this basic cosmological framework, Ptolemy added detailed mathematical theories for the motion of every planet. With some slight adjustments, these theories were sufficient to predict the planets' motions pretty well up until Kepler's time.

Ptolemy's cosmology was consistent with Aristotle's much older theory of the elements. Aristotle, the great and influential Greek philosopher of the fourth century B.C., had taught that the heavens are made up of a substance called

aether. Unlike the earthly elements, earth, air, fire, and water, whose natural motions were finite (toward and away from the center of the earth), the heavenly aether alone had a natural, unending circular motion.

In the 50 years since Copernicus published his heliocentric system in 1543, not many people seriously entertained the possibility that it might be true. It was too unbelievable that the earth should move without us sensing it. Just the earth's daily rotation would have to be a dizzying 900 miles per hour, not counting its annual motion around the sun. And yet objects fell straight down, not away from the direction of the earth's rotation, and birds and objects in the air did not fall behind as the earth rotated out from underneath them. The motion of the earth seemed physically impossible. Ptolemy's geocentric system, on the other hand, was perfectly consistent with Aristotle's physics.

In the second half of the sixteenth century, however, problems had arisen with the theory of the aether. According to Aristotle, aether was unchanging and immutable. But in 1572, a dazzling *nova,* or "new star," appeared. Careful observations showed that it was not below the moon in the earthly region but somewhere high in the aether. And then came the magnificent comet of 1577.

While Kepler was holding his mother's hand on the hill outside Leonberg, far to the north on the Island of Hven, the Danish nobleman Tycho Brahe (who, like Galileo and Michelangelo, is known by his first name) had made exhaustive, precise observations of the comet. They showed that it, too, was above the moon, not just below the moon in the realm of fire where comets had been thought to be. In addition, the comet was moving somewhere through regions thought to be full of aether spheres. In 1588, after 11 years of patient preparation, Tycho declared with meticulous justification that the aether spheres did not exist. It was not enough for him to become a Copernican—the physical absurdity of heliocentrism and the testimony of Holy Scripture stood in the way—but the Ptolemaic system was under threat.

For Kepler, studying under Maestlin in the early 1590s, the physical objections to a moving earth seemed a small thing. For him, the Copernican system had a wider, religious significance. The universe, as he saw it, was nothing less than the image of God, its Creator. The sun, the most resplendent body, was situated in the center, whence it distributed light, heat, and motion to the planets. It represented God the Father. Outermost in the system were the stars. They were located on a fixed sphere—the most perfect of geometrical bodies—centered on the sun that enclosed the universe and defined its space. It represented God the Son, Jesus Christ. A sphere is generated by an infinite number of

text continues on page 22

COPERNICUS'S MODEL OF RETROGRADE MOTION

Nicolaus Copernicus published his heliocentric system in 1543, the year of his death.

In Ptolemy's geocentric system, the earth was at rest in the center of the universe, and all the motions we see in the heavens were attributed to the stars and planets. In Copernicus's heliocentric system, many of the motions are attributed to the motion of the earth, our vantage point. It is just as if you are in a train at the station: when you look out the window at another train and it starts to move, it is not immediately clear whether it is your train or the other that is moving. For instance, according to Copernicus, the daily motion all celestial bodies share—rising in the east and setting in the west—is really caused by the eastward rotation of the earth on its axis. The heavens do not move over us; we move under them.

The situation with our view of another planet is more complicated, because both the earth and the planet have their own motion around the sun, and our perception of the planet's location depends on both where the earth is and where the planet is. Mars is a good example. Much of the time, we perceive Mars's motion as it moves slowly eastward with respect to background stars. But when the earth and Mars are on the same side of the sun, the earth passes Mars because the earth travels faster and its orbit is smaller. As the earth moves by, our motion makes Mars look like it is falling behind. And during that period of time, from the earth it looks like Mars stops moving and even moves backward for a time.

text continued from page 20

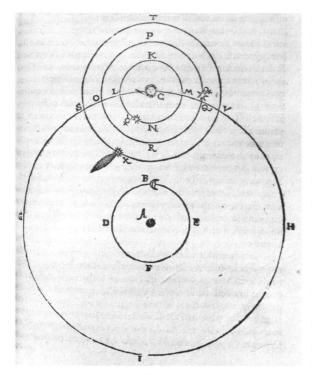

This is Tycho Brahe's diagram of the location of the Comet of 1577 from his book De mundi aetherei recentioribus phaenomenis (*On the More Recent Phenomena of the Aetherial World*) (1588). The comet is moving around the sun on the path marked XVTS near Venus, which moves on the path QPOR. Mercury is innermost, on path NMKL.

equal straight lines coming forth from its center, which fill out the space between the sphere and its center. This intervening space represented the Holy Spirit. As in the Trinitarian concept of God, in which Father, Son, and Holy Spirit unite in the one God, so in the sphere, no one of the elements—center, surface, or volume—can exist without the others. The periods of the planets and their distances also made sense in the Copernican arrangement: the closer they are to the sun, the source of all change and motion, the faster they move around. During his time at the University of Tübingen, Kepler defended the reality of the Copernican system in two separate formal academic debates, using just this type of argument. But he always considered astronomy and the Copernican system to be just a side interest to his religious studies.

In the meantime, Kepler's theological studies were proceeding according to schedule. On August 11, 1591, he completed his required two-year advanced study in the arts and received his master's degree. Two months later, the university senate wrote to the mayor and city council of Weil der Stadt requesting that his scholarship be renewed. "Young Kepler," they wrote, "has such an extraordinary and splendid intellect that something special can be expected from him."

In early 1594, however, came a devastating change of plans. Within months of completing an additional three years of theological studies, Kepler was forced to cut them off. The previous year, Georg Stadius, the mathematics teacher at a

Protestant seminary school in Graz, Styria (a district of Austria), had passed away. In November, the Styrian representatives appealed to the prominent Lutheran University of Tübingen to recommend a replacement, preferably one who also knew history and Greek. Kepler had distinguished himself in his enthusiastic study with Maestlin and had otherwise done well, so the theological faculty selected him.

It was a bitter personal struggle, as Kepler was torn between his calling and his duty. Previously, when his friends at the *Stift* had received far-flung postings, they had complained openly and attempted to avoid them. Seeing this, Kepler resolved that when the call came to him, he would accept it promptly and with dignity. Now his smugness came back to haunt him. It was not so much that Graz was far away in a foreign country that bothered him but rather that he was being taken away from the chance to be a pastor and serve the church. He did not want to be in the lowly position of a mathematics teacher. On top of that, he did not see that he had any particular aptitude in mathematics. On the other hand, he did not want to be selfish; one is not put in this world for himself alone. Finally, he proposed a compromise that left open the possibility that he could return to church service in the future.

The paperwork was quickly put in place. The head of the Tübingen *Stift*, and the inspectors of the Protestant school in Graz wrote to the duke of Württemberg requesting permission for Kepler to leave Württemberg and take up the job. The duke signed off on March 5. Kepler hurriedly tied up his affairs in Tübingen. On March 13, 1594, he left his beloved university for far-off Styria.

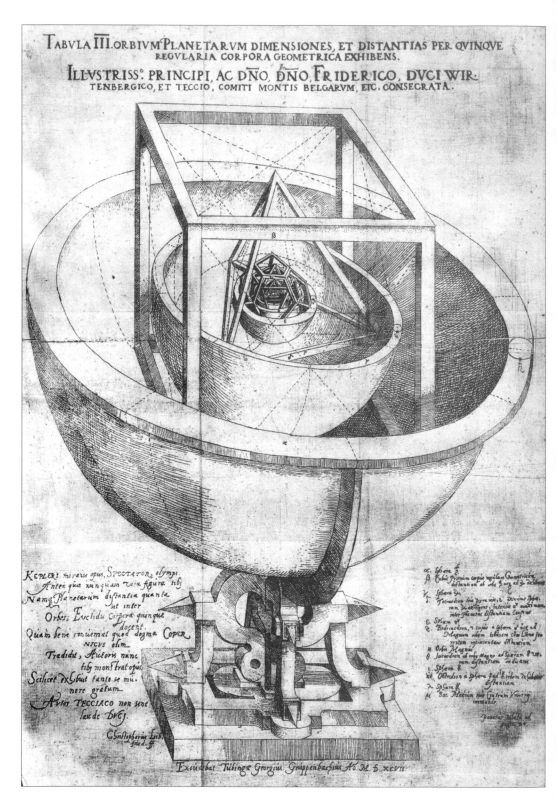

Kepler's cosmological hypothesis from the Mysterium cosmographicum (1596) provides a geometrical explanation of the distances between the planets in their orbits..

The Secret of the Universe

It took Kepler nearly a month to travel from Württemberg, through Bavaria, into Austria, and then across Austria toward its southern frontier. On April 11, 1594, he reached the hilltop fortress town of Graz, the capital of Styria, one of the districts of Inner Austria. He ascended the narrow streets and found the squat, square building housing the Protestant college, where he was shown into the colonnaded courtyard and taken to his new lodging.

The long journey underscored the remoteness of the place and the foreignness of his new situation. The most significant change was the charged religious climate in which he found himself. Unlike Württemberg, which was staunchly Lutheran, in Styria, Catholics and Protestants lived side by side in uneasy coexistence. Ideally, this situation should never have come to pass. Under the terms of the Religious Peace of Augsburg, Styria should have been Catholic like its Hapsburg rulers. Decreeing the practice of religion, however, required the power to enforce it, and almost all of the powerful land-owning nobility in Inner Austria had converted to Lutheranism. Twenty years before, Archduke Charles had granted the Protestant nobility the concession under the Pacification of Bruck (1578) that Protestant nobles in the countryside and Protestant citizens of cities like Graz could freely exercise their religion. Almost ever since, there had existed a religious stalemate.

Kepler's position in this conflict was not neutral. The Protestant seminary school had been set up in 1574 in deliberate opposition to the Catholic Jesuit college founded the previous year. It had developed into the principal seat of the Protestant party in Graz, and its staff were important representatives of the Protestant community.

There were four preachers and about a dozen teachers at the all-male school, which comprised two levels, a boy's school and an upper school. Kepler taught in the philosophical division of the highest of the four classes in the upper school. Though he was called to teach advanced mathematics, which included astronomy, his classes were not well attended. His first year, he had only a few students, and the second, none at all. The school inspectors realized that it

Matthäus Merian created this view of Graz, the capital of Stryia, for the Topographia. In addition to his work as a schoolteacher, Kepler was the district mathematician of Styria.

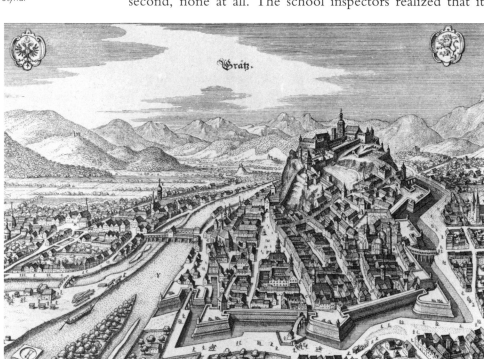

was the subject matter and not their new young professor that was at fault. Instead, Kepler was reassigned to teach other topics, and, during the following years, taught a variety of courses, including rhetoric, Virgil, basic arithmetic, history, and ethics.

In addition to his duties as a schoolteacher, Kepler carried the joint appointment of district mathematician. As such, it was his duty to compile an annual calendar and astrological prognostication, a prediction for the coming year. Throughout his life, Kepler had mixed feelings about astrology. On the one hand, as he wrote a few years later in his book *De fundamentis astrologiae certioribus* (On the More Certain Principles of Astrology) (1601), he disliked the idea of "nourishing the superstition of fatheads." On the other hand, he sincerely believed that alignments of the planets had subtle but important influences on man and nature. Kepler seems to have struck the right balance for his *Prognostication for 1595*. In his first prognostication, he predicted bitter cold, an attack by the Turks on Austria's southern flank, and a peasant uprising. That winter was so cold, it was said, that shepherds in the mountains broke off their noses when they blew them. Kepler's other unpleasant prophesies came true as well. He was an instant success.

Of course, Kepler had another motivation for composing pubic prognostications and for the private astrological consulting he did: it was a valuable source of income. As he wrote justifying his astrological activities to his disapproving former professor Michael Maestlin, "If God gave every animal tools for maintaining life, what harm is there if for the same purpose He joined astrology to astronomy?" For his prognostication for 1595, Kepler received a bonus of 20 florins, worth seven weeks of his 150 florin salary as a teacher. His subsequent annual prognostications were regularly rewarded in the same way.

Kepler had accepted the assignment to teach mathematics in Graz more or less unwillingly. He resolved, however, now

that he was a professional mathematician—or an astronomer, which was really the same thing then—to elevate his studies to a suitably philosophic level. He began by reconsidering Copernicus's heliocentric system of the world, and he noticed that there were some unexplained elements in it.

One of the most satisfying features of the heliocentric system had been that it fit the orbits of the planets together into a harmonious, commensurable system. That is to say, Copernicus's heliocentric system required that the planets be located at precise distances relative to the earth, so the distances of all of the planets from the sun were determined with respect to one another, or the system was "commensurable." In the old Ptolemaic cosmology, the relative distance of the planets had been determined simply by stacking up the systems of spheres belonging to the different planets one on top of another, like the layers of an onion. But in Copernicus's heliocentric system, the planets all had to be located at specific distances from the sun. Mercury's orbit had to be about one third the size of the earth's, Venus about two thirds, Mars about one and a half, Jupiter five times, and Saturn ten times.

As Kepler began looking more closely at the heliocentric system, he realized that Copernicus had offered no fundamental reason why the planets were located at these particular distances. Kepler began to wonder, why these particular distances? For that matter, why were there six and only six planets? Or, as Kepler considered the question, why did God choose to construct the solar system in this way and not another?

The basis for an answer to these questions came to him while he was in front of his class teaching on July 19, 1595, when he drew a diagram of an equilateral triangle inscribed within a circle, so that the vertices of the triangle just touched the surrounding circle. He noticed that if he inscribed another circle within the triangle, so that it just touched the midpoints of the sides of the surrounding triangle, the ratio of the size of the large circle to the small circle was about the same as the relative size of Saturn's orbit to Jupiter's orbit. If he then inscribed a square within the inner circle and incribed a smaller circle within it, its size relative to the other circles might be the same as Mars's orbit to Saturn's and Jupiter's orbit. He immediately began to suspect that the relative sizes of all of the planets' orbits had some such geometrical basis, that God had used geometry as an archetype while creating the universe.

text continues on page 31

I n Greek antiquity, it was already known that there are five and only five regular polyhedra, that is, three-dimensional geometrical figures with all identical equilateral faces, which are also called "Platonic" solids. A cube is the most common example of a regular solid. How can one tell that there are four and only four possible others?

Start by thinking about how one might construct a regular solid, starting with the sides around one point. There have to be at least three sides; otherwise, a three-dimensional body cannot be formed. Arrange three squares around a point, and then fold them up to form a three-sided figure, which is half a cube. An identical figure attached to the first will complete the cube with six sides. Equilateral triangles will fold up more tightly, leaving a space at the top the same size as the other sides. Attach one more side, and one has a tetrahedron with four faces. Pentagons will fold up like a shallow dish, but additional pentagons can be attached to the edges. If one adds more sides to these and then more sides to the next set of edges, a dodecahedron with twelve identical pentagonal faces eventually will be formed. Hexagonal faces will not work. Three hexagons meet in a flush plane, and they cannot be folded up to form the sides of a solid.

If we go back to triangles, we see that we could try four equilateral triangles around a point. Fold them up, and one has a pyramid shape. An identical pyramid joined to the top forms a regular octahedron with eight faces. Five equilateral triangles will also fit around a point. Fold them up, and the figure is very shallow, but if one keeps adding on sides, a regular twenty-sided icosahedron eventually will be formed. Six equilateral triangles will form a flush plane which cannot be folded into a three-dimensional figure. Four squares will also form a flush plane. Nor can any other combination of regular polygons be fit around a single point. Therefore, these are the only possible regular solids.

text continued from page 65

The use of plane geometry was unsatisfactory, and he quickly realized that he would have to use solid geometry. The universe is three dimensional, after all. With three dimensions, he would have to work with spheres instead of circles and regular solids instead of polygons. It had been known to mathematicians since antiquity that there are five and only five regular solids, the tetrahedron (four-sided), the cube (six-sided), the octahedron (eight-sided), the dodecahedron (twelve-sided), and the icosahedron (twenty-sided). As soon as Kepler remembered that, the answer became clear to him. Later, in the Preface to his book *Mysterium cosmographicum*, he quoted the proposition just as it had come to him at that moment:

> The earth's circle is the measure of all things. Circumscribe a dodecahedron around it. The circle surrounding it will be Mars. Circumscribe a tetrahedron around Mars. The circle surrounding it will be Jupiter. Circumscribe a cube around Jupiter. The surrounding circle will be Saturn. Now, inscribe an icosahedron inside the earth. The circle inscribed in it will be Venus. Inscribe an octahedron inside Venus. The circle inscribed in it will be Mercury.

This detail of a plate from Kepler's Harmonice mundi shows the construction of the Platonic solids: the tetrahedron (top left), the octahedron (Oo), icosahedron (Pp), cube (Qq), and dodecahedron (Rr).

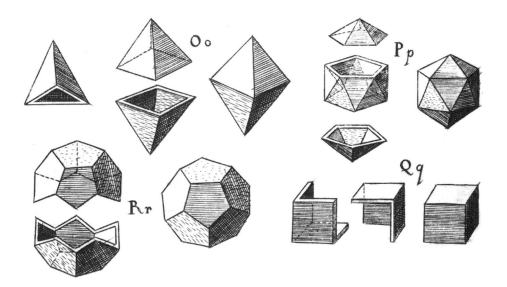

The spacing of the planets within the polyhedra seemed just about right. More importantly, Kepler knew immediately why there are six and only six planets. Since there were only five possible regular polyhedra, they could be inscribed between only six different spheres. The discovery he made on July 20, 1595, was so profound he wept tears of joy. As he wrote in a letter to Maestlin, he regarded his discoveries as "stupendous miracles of God."

By October 1595, Kepler had resolved to publish his findings in a book. It would be, as he saw it, a physical proof of the truth of Copernicus's heliocentric system and, at the same time, a testament to God's glory. In so making known God's plan of the world, Kepler found a way to make meaningful the assignment he had been given to become a mathematician. As he wrote in a letter to Maestlin at the beginning of October,

> I am in haste to publish, dearest teacher, but not for my benefit . . . I am devoting my effort so that these things can be published as quickly as possible for the glory of God, who wants to be recognized from the Book of Nature . . . Just as I pledged myself to God, so my intention remains. I wanted to be a theologian, and for a while I was anguished. But now, see how, God is also glorified in astronomy through my work.

There would be many details to be ironed out before he was ready. Among other things, there was another fundamental question about the Copernican system to address: why did the planets have their particular periods? Here, Kepler's thinking took a very important turn. Ever since he was a student, he had thought that the reason the nearer planets go around faster was their proximity to the sun, which is somehow the source of the force that makes them go around. Now, he tried to derive a mathematical formula based on his physical intuition that would relate the planets' periods to their distances. There were two effects to take into account. The first is just geometry: the further a planet is from the sun, the longer its orbit will be and the longer it will take to get around. But in addition, the further away it is, the weaker the planet-moving force will be. So he added these effects to come up with the formula: from one planet to another, the increase in the period will be twice the difference of their distances. He himself later realized the formula was incorrect, but remarkably it yielded planetary distances that were similar to those derived from the polyhedral hypothesis. Again, he wept tears of joy and excitedly wrote to Maestlin about his new hypothesis, "Behold how near the truth I have come!"

Kepler sent his first outline of the two main arguments he would include in his book to Maestlin in October 1595. Throughout that cold winter, he filled out that outline with a number of auxiliary arguments. Since the polyhedral hypothesis was founded on the idea that God had rationally structured the universe based on the five regular solids, Kepler turned his attention to seeing what meaning he could discern in the particular arrangement of the solids. In the process, he ended up having a lot more to say about the polyhedral hypothesis than the planet-moving force hypothesis, but he did come up with one additional argument based on the planet-moving force hypothesis that would be extremely influential in his later thinking about planetary theory.

Around March 1596, when he was putting the finishing touches on his manuscript, he noticed a very interesting application of the planet-moving force hypothesis. Previously, he had only seen the planet-moving force as a way to relate the periods and distances of different planets to one another. After some more thought, he realized that it could be applied to a single planet as it moved on its own orbit around the sun. As the planet approached nearer to the sun, the planet-moving force would be stronger and the planet would move more quickly. Later on in its orbit, as it receded from the sun, the force would be weaker and the planet would slow down. This general change of speed of a planet with its distance from the sun had been built into

Ptolemy's and Copernicus's mathematical models of the motion of the planets, but neither of them had interpreted this change in speed physically.

This idea was, in fact, the single element of the book that would worry Maestlin. He later admonished Kepler not to make too much of this planet-moving force hypothesis "lest it should lead to the ruin of astronomy." What troubled Maestlin was that Kepler seemed to be trampling on a delicate division line between two parts of astronomy. In the sixteenth century, astronomy was widely regarded to consist of a physical part, which dealt with the nature and structure of the universe, otherwise known as cosmology, and a mathematical part, devoted to producing accurate mathematical theories of the planets' motion. Everything else in Kepler's book seemed to fall into the physical part. But by saying that his planet-moving force could explain certain mathematical details of Ptolemy's and Copernicus's planetary theories, Kepler seemed to be importing physical reasoning into mathematical astronomy. As far as Maestlin was concerned, it seemed this would only mess up the theories of the planets.

In January 1596, Kepler received word from home that both his grandfathers were ailing, and at the end of the month, he left Graz to visit them. Sadly, old Sebald died during his visit home. While Kepler was in Württemberg, he took the opportunity to promote his new hypotheses. In February, he traveled up to the capital, Stuttgart, to try his luck at the ducal court.

The aristocracy were patrons of science and the arts generally, but Kepler had a curiosity to market: a model of his new system of nested polyhedra in silver. Or, if something really splashy was desired, Kepler outlined how the model could be realized in the form of a huge punch bowl. The spaces between the different planetary spheres could be filled with various beverages, and by means of hidden pipes and valves, the party guests could fill their glasses from seven taps spaced around the rim. The duke was skeptical at first, but after seeing a paper model Kepler had painstakingly constructed and consulting with his astronomical expert (Maestlin), he advanced Kepler some money to fabricate the more restrained silver model.

The next three months were a frustrating disaster. Kepler was stuck in Stuttgart pestering the goldsmith, and the project hardly got anywhere. In the end, he had to go back to Styria, leaving the project in the goldsmith's hands. Although the matter dragged out for a few years, the entertaining model of Kepler's polyhedra was never built. It would have been wondrous to see.

In the meantime, Kepler had the opportunity to travel to Tübingen, visit with Maestlin, and begin negotiations with a printer to publish his book. None of the printers back in Graz were competent to print a complex astronomical book, but Tübingen had a serious printer named Gruppenbach. Gruppenbach agreed to publish the book on condition that it be approved by the university senate. The senate asked Maestlin for his expert opinion of the astronomical content, and he responded enthusiastically. The only part that the theological faculty demanded to be removed was Kepler's chapter on how to reconcile heliocentrism with passages in the bible that seemed to support geocentrism, such as Psalm 104:5, which states that God "laid the foundations of the earth that it should not be removed for ever." The real meaning of Holy Scripture was not Kepler's business. As he was admonished in a letter from Matthias Hafenreffer, a professor of theology, Kepler was to restrict himself to "playing the part of the abstract mathematician." It was frustrating to Kepler, since he had conceived his work as a physical proof of the truth of heliocentrism. How was he to glorify God speaking only hypothetically? But he obediently went along with the Lutheran authorities.

When Kepler returned to Graz in August 1596, there was some damage to repair from his long absence. To begin with, he had received leave for two months, and he had

These miniature portraits of Johannes Kepler and his wife Barbara date from around the time of their wedding in 1597.

been absent for seven. But he carried a letter from the duke of Württemberg asking for Kepler's superiors' forgiveness since Kepler had been delayed in his service. This was excuse enough. Unfortunately, Kepler's neglect of his love life would not prove so easy to repair.

As early as the previous December, Kepler had made the acquaintance of a young woman with whom he quickly fell in love. Her name was Barbara Müller. Among other things, we know that she was pretty, plump, and extremely fond of cooked tortoise. She was the eldest daughter of a wealthy mill owner and entrepreneur, Jobst Müller, who resided on an estate about two hours south of Graz. Although she was only 23, Barbara had recently become a widow for the second time. Both of Barbara's previous husbands had been significantly older than she was—both were 40—which was not an uncommon state of affairs in days when family and community played so great a role in determining whom one was to marry. An older man would have shown his capacity to be a success and to provide for his family. By contrast, Kepler was scarcely 24 when he began to woo her. Although he had a university education, he was still only a schoolteacher with unknown prospects. It would not prove easy to convince Herr Müller that Kepler was a suitable match for her. Herr Müller was a businessman who kept his eye on the bottom line. Barbara had financial assets. Kepler was a penniless scholar.

Probably as early as January 1596, a delegation of respectable members of the Protestant community was assembled to present and recommend Kepler to Jobst Müller as a suitor for Barbara. Kepler left his matrimonial affairs in their hands when he left for his long trip to Württemberg. In June, during his stay there, he received word that they had been successful. He was advised to hurry home, but not before purchasing silk (or at least double taffeta) wedding clothes for himself and his fiancee on the way in Ulm.

As Kepler's failing attempt to construct the model of his celestial discovery dragged out through the summer, the arrangements for the wedding also fell through. In his absence, Herr Müller had become convinced that he could do better for his daughter. When Kepler returned in the fall, he learned that his longed-for union had been canceled. Fortunately, he received support from his school and church, which weighed in on his behalf. Before he had left for Württemberg, he had given Barbara his word. By the middle of January, Kepler appealed to the church: either it must get involved and convince Barbara's father, or Kepler needed to be released from his promise. In short order, the church had set things right again. A solemn promise of marriage was celebrated on February 9 and the wedding on April 27, 1597.

For a while at least, joy reigned supreme in the Kepler household. Kepler received a silver cup as a wedding gift from the school authorities, as well as a raise of 50 florins, to 200 florins a year, to accommodate his move out of the school grounds. Kepler loved his seven-year-old stepdaughter Regina. Barbara quickly became pregnant and bore him a son on February 2, 1598. He was christened Heinrich, Kepler's father's and brother's name. Kepler cast a horoscope for his firstborn son. He would be like his father, only better—charming, noble in character, nimble of body and mind, with mathematical and mechanical aptitude. It was a crushing blow when after only two months of life, his little son Heinrich became ill and passed away. "The passage of time does not lessen my wife's grief," Kepler wrote, quoting Ecclesiastes, "the passage strikes at my heart: 'O vanity of vanities, and all is vanity.'"

The first happy days of Kepler's marriage saw the arrival of the first copies of his book, whose complicated printing was not finished until March 1597. Although the volume was slim, its title was long. It read *Prodromus dissertationum cosmographicarum, continens mysterium cosmographicum, de admirabili proportione orbium coelestium, deque causis coelorum numeri, magnitudinis, motuumque periodicorum genuinis & proprijs, demonstratum per quinque regularia corpora geometrica*, or in English, The Forerunner of Cosmographical Essays, Containing the Cosmographical Secret: On the Marvelous Proportion of the Celestial Spheres, and on the True and Particular Causes of the Number, Size, and Periodic Motions of the Heavens, Demonstrated by Means of the Five Regular Geometric Bodies. It is known by the abbreviated Latin title, the *Mysterium cosmographicum*, which translates roughly as The Secret of the Universe. Kepler called it a "forerunner" because he foresaw writing a series of treatises on the Copernican system. This book contained his premier discovery, and so he wanted to get it out first and see how people responded to it.

He now began sending copies of the book to astronomers for their opinions. The two copies he dispatched blindly to Italy found their way into the hands of a then little-known mathematics professor at the University of Padua. The man confided to Kepler in a letter that he too had been a Copernican for many years and had been collecting physical proofs of the motion of the earth but had kept them to himself, "terrified as I am by the fortune of our teacher Copernicus himself, who although he earned

Prodròmus

DISSERTATIONVM COSMOGRA-
PHICARVM, CONTINENS MYSTE-
RIVM COSMOGRAPHI-
CVM,

DE ADMIRABILI

PROPORTIONE ORBIVM
COELESTIVM, DEQVE CAVSIS
cœlorum numeri, magnitudinis, motuumque periodicorum genuinis & pro-
prijs,

DEMONSTRATVM, PER QVINQVE
regularia corpora Geometrica,

A

M. IOANNE KEPLERO, VVIRTEM-
bergico, Illustrium Styriæ prouincia-
lium Mathematico.

Quotidiè morior, fateorque: sed inter Olympi
Dum tenet assiduas me mea cura vias:
Non pedibus terram contingo: sed ante Tonantem
Nectare, diuina pascor & ambrosiâ.

Addita est erudita NARRATIO M. GEORGII IOACHIMI
RHETICI, *de Libris Reuolutionum, atq̃, admirandis de numero, or-*
dine, & distantijs Sphærarum Mundi hypothesibus, excellentissimi Ma-
thematici, totiusq̃, Astronomia Restauratoris D. NICOLAI
COPERNICI.

TVBINGÆ
Excudebat Georgius Gruppenbachius,
ANNO M. D. XCVI.

The title page of the first edition of the Mysterium cosmographicum *carries the publication date 1596 (MDXCVI),* although the printing was not finished until 1597.

This is the cosmological system of Tycho Brahe from his book De mundi aetherei recentioribus phaenomenis (On the More Recent Phenomena of the Aetherial World). The earth is stationary at the center of the sphere of fixed stars (the outermost sphere). The moon and the sun circle the earth (the center of the diagram), but the planets circle the sun.

DE COMETA ANNI 1577.   189

NOVA MVNDANI SYSTEMATIS HYPOTYPOSIS ab Authore nuper adinuenta,qua tum vetus illa Ptolemaica redundantia & inconcinnitas, tum etiam recens Coperniana in motu Terræ Physica absurditas, excluduntur, omniaq, Apparentiis Cælestibus aptißime correspondent.

immortal fame among some, nevertheless among a vast number (for such is the number of fools) appeared fit to be ridiculed and hissed off the stage." Kepler was especially tickled by the unknown man's name. His first name was the same as his last, like an echo: Galileo Galilei. Kepler urged Galileo to come out publicly in support of Copernicus. "Have confidence, Galileo," he wrote, "and step forward. If I guess correctly, few of Europe's principal mathematicians will want to distance themselves from us; so great a force is truth." But for the time being, Galileo kept silent. Kepler would not hear from him again for many years.

Kepler next became involved in a scandal and a bitter dispute, which he would desperately regret but which did much to shape his future. One of the people who asked for a copy of the book was the emperor's mathematician, Nicholas Reimer, who used the Latin last name Ursus, meaning "bear." Kepler had written to Ursus a year and a half earlier relating his discovery, but he had never written back. Now, suddenly, Ursus was interested. What Kepler did not know was that Ursus was planning to use him as a pawn in his vicious intellectual dispute with the Danish nobleman Tycho Brahe, Europe's leading astronomer. Both men were claiming to have invented a new cosmological system. It was like Copernicus's system in that the planets went around the sun, but to keep the earth unmoved at the center, the sun moved around the earth with all of the planets in train. In his earlier letter, as a way of being nice and without really knowing what he was saying, Kepler had written "I love your hypotheses." Ursus planned to reprint Kepler's letter in his own book *On Astronomical Hypotheses* (1597) to make it look like Kepler was on his side.

Ursus was a coarse man, the son of illiterate pig herders, who had worked his way up from the filth to become mathematician to the emperor. He was not going to let Tycho Brahe, a privileged aristocrat, accuse him of stealing his idea. On the title page of *On Astronomical Hypotheses*, Ursus printed a motto, a pun on his name, which read "I shall meet them as a bear separated from her cubs." As the motto suggested, it was a wild attack. He crossed every line of civility, making lewd suggestions about Tycho's family and insinuating that Tycho had recently left Denmark because he had committed a horrible crime. In the end, Tycho managed to round up most of the copies and burn them. Only a handful of copies survived the flames.

In the meantime, Kepler was innocently trying to send a copy of his book to Tycho Brahe, whose opinion he was anxious to know. Tycho had moved to northern Germany and it took a long time for Kepler's letter to catch up to him. By a fateful coincidence, it finally arrived on the very same day as Ursus's horrible new book. Tycho was not normally an even-tempered man. For once, however, he reacted with moderation. He could not imagine, he wrote, that Kepler had known his letter would be used in Ursus's "defamatory and criminal publication." For his part, Tycho only wanted a statement of Kepler's opinion of Ursus's behavior, which he could use in his planned lawsuit against Ursus.

With regard to Kepler's book, Tycho mentioned that he had glanced at it and he thought Kepler's speculation was ingenious, but that Copernicus's values for the planetary distances were not accurate enough for his purpose. But he suggested Kepler might make good use of the collection of accurate observations he had amassed over his lifetime as an astronomer. It was a tantalizing possibility. From that moment on, Kepler knew that he would have to meet Tycho face-to-face. Following roundabout routes, their exchange of letters had taken over a year. If he was ever going to straighten out this disaster involving Ursus, he would have to see Tycho in person.

Even as it was becoming clear to Kepler that he needed to confer with Tycho Brahe regarding his research, other events were afoot in Styria that pushed him into Tycho's arms. Shortly after his marriage, Kepler had remarked to Maestlin that, because of his wife's extensive holdings and family connections, he was now effectively bound to Styria, unless "the land was no longer safe for a Lutheran." He had reason to have such concerns. A few months earlier, Archduke Ferdinand II had come of age and assumed rule over Inner Austria, the part of Austria which included Styria. Although his father Archduke Charles had tolerated the Protestants in his lands, Ferdinand's mother had been fervently Catholic and had tried to reverse his concessions. Ferdinand had been raised in Catholic Bavaria and educated at Ingolstadt under the direction of Jesuit advisors. It was feared that he would make good the threat to enforce his rights under the Peace of Augsburg and force all people in his lands to share his Catholic faith. The fear was not misplaced.

There was tension early in Kepler's time in Graz, but the new prince made no overt hostile move. Only after a meeting with Pope Clement VIII in Rome in the summer of 1598, during which, the story went, he vowed to return his lands to Catholicism, did he begin taking measures against the Protestants. The Protestants viewed his return from Italy with apprehension. It was rumored that he would return at the head of an army of Italian soldiers.

When Ferdinand returned, with tension high, there were incidents between the Catholics and Protestants. The balance of power had long been in the Protestant hands. They did not sense the shift underway and brashly taunted the Catholics. Kepler watched in despair as his people brought on their own ruin. Rude caricatures of the Pope were distributed. A Protestant preacher in the pulpit ridiculed the worship of Mary with an obscene gesture. Arrests were made. Poor Protestants in the hospital were refused care, and Protestants were overtaxed for burials.

Then came the beginning of the end. The Catholic archpriest, the highest-ranking priest in the city, forbade the practice of every Protestant sacrament, including communion and marriage. The Protestants appealed to the archduke, and it only made things worse. On September 13, 1598, he decreed that the Protestant college and all church and school ministries were to be dissolved within 14 days. Ten days later, the archbishop ordered all Protestant ministers and teachers to leave the city within a week, under penalty of death. Again, the Protestants protested; they summoned the assembly of the Estates of Styria, and the counselors anxiously begged the prince to repeal the decree. Instead, he issued a stunning new order. On September 28, 1598, he decreed that all the collegiate preachers, rectors, and school employees had to leave the city of Graz and its environs by nightfall, that they then had to clear out of Styria altogether within the previously given deadline of one week, and that any of them who showed themselves

again faced "the loss of life and limb." Kepler and his col-
leagues were banished. They hastily gathered together some
supplies, and leaving their wives behind, they dispersed out
of the city into the countryside. They hoped for a future
reprieve, but only Kepler was ever allowed to return.

At the end of October, Kepler's petition to be allowed to
return was granted, and he came from wherever he had been
sheltering back into the city. Because he held the dual job of
mathematics teacher and district mathematician, he was
allowed to return in the latter capacity, as his friends and sup-
porters had pleaded. For the time being, Kepler was safe.

The screw continued to turn on the Protestants in Graz,
as they were forbidden the practice of their religion. At first,
they simply left the city to attend services at the country
estates of noblemen whose Protestant clergy had not been
expelled, but soon that was prohibited. Protestants were
required to have their children baptized as Catholics and to
marry in the Catholic ceremony. A grief-stricken Kepler
confronted these oppressive measures after the death of his
second child, a daughter named Susanna who was born in
June 1599 but lived only 35 days. He refused a Catholic bur-
ial for her and was fined. He appealed, and the fine was
halved, but he still had to pay before the dead infant could
be buried. Luther's German translation of the Bible and all
"heretical" books were banned. Searches were undertaken
and guards were set at the gates to keep them out. In a spectacular display, 10,000 seized books were burned in a huge
bonfire in Graz.

Relieved of his teaching duties, Kepler escaped from the
tumult in the streets to his heavenly speculations, developing
thoughts on the harmony of the heavens that he would only
publish some twenty years later. But he kept his eyes open for
an avenue of escape. He inquired about the possibility of an
appointment at the University of Tübingen without success.
He learned that Tycho had become the emperor's new mathematician, making a triumphant entrance into Prague while

Ursus fled the city. In December, Tycho reissued the invitation to Kepler to come join him for astronomical consultations. When the opportunity arose at the beginning of January 1600 to travel to Prague in the company of Baron Johann Friedrich Hoffmann free of charge, Kepler jumped at the chance. He was on his way before Tycho's second invitation even arrived.

This portrait depicts Tycho Brahe in 1586, at the age of 46. On the arch around him are the crests of important noble families to which he was related.

The New Astronomy

On January 11, 1600, Kepler set off from Graz to meet Tycho Brahe. After a journey of about ten days, the party arrived in Prague, the seat of the Holy Roman Emperor. High on the hill overlooking the city sat the Hradschin, the emperor's sprawling compound incorporating castle, cathedral, palace, and imperial offices. Clustered around it, as though drawn to the seat of power, were the palaces of aristocrats and ambassadors in the district called Hradcany. The Lesser Town, home of courtiers and craftsmen, spilled down the hillside to the Molda. Across the long stone bridge, the city spread out into the patrician Old Town, and further into New Town. Compared to Graz, it was a busy and chaotic place, with numerous open markets among the city's narrow, stinking streets. Prague was an important city in its own right as capital of prosperous Bohemia. But the presence of the emperor had also attracted a diverse international community of ambassadors, aristocrats, power-seekers, and hangers-on, as well as scholars, alchemists, artists, and skilled craftsmen.

Tycho did not live in the city but in Benatky castle in the countryside northeast of the city, which had been put at his disposal by the emperor. Consequently, it took some time before Kepler could send out a note announcing his presence in Prague. The next day, Tycho sent his son, Tycho Jr., and a trusted associate, Franz Tengnagel, into town with instructions to bring Kepler back out with them in the carriage.

The meeting of Johannes Kepler and Tycho Brahe on February 4, 1600, is extraordinarily significant in the history of science. The two men could not have been more different. Tycho was a nobleman, self-assured, domineering, and combative. Kepler was a commoner, sincere, reflective, peace-loving, and unassuming. Yet they fit together like a lock and key. Tycho was the observer, with a lifetime's accomplishment behind him in the form of 20 volumes of astronomical observations stretching back more than 35 years. Kepler was the young theorist, with one slim, highly speculative volume to his credit. Both were brilliant, and each one's skills complemented the other's. But neither was there by choice. Tycho had abandoned his native Denmark after a haughty dispute with his patron the king, and now was an expatriate, if not an exile. Kepler had fled oppressive atmosphere of religious intolerance in Styria. The bringing together of these two men at this place and time would change astronomy.

Tycho Brahe was an unusual man, to say the least. The first thing that would have struck Kepler about him was that he had a prosthetic nose made of gold and silver blended to a flesh color, a souvenir of a duel dating back to Tycho's student days. He had close-cropped, receding reddish hair, with a trim beard overhung by a large handlebar mustache. His personality was regal and overbearing.

Tycho had been born into the highest level of Danish society, a small class of aristocratic families that owned and ran the country. With the lavish support of the Danish crown, he had established an unprecedented observatory, Uraniborg, and engaged scores of scholars and craftsmen to aid him in his investigations of the heavens. Tycho had spent

most of the last twenty years holed up on his private island
devoting his attention—and a great deal of the king of
Denmark's gold—to a total reformation of astronomical
theory founded on an unprecedentedly complete and accurate collection of observations of the planets. He had trained
assistants, cultivated instrument makers, and sent agents to
collect astronomical books and manuscripts. Then, just
when his 20 years of astronomical activity seemed to be
coming to fruition, his royal support had suddenly eroded
and he had had to leave Denmark in search of a new patron.
After a couple years of uncertainty, he had secured the support of a most important and devoted patron, the Holy
Roman Emperor Rudolf II.

When Kepler arrived, Benatky castle was abuzz with
activity. Tycho was never comfortable without his great
astronomical instruments set up, and masons and carpenters
were in the process of making modifications to the castle to
accommodate them. Interconnected instrument bays were
being erected along the bluff overlooking the river Iser and
the flat plain to the south. Here, he would regather his
forces and found a "New Uraniborg."

A large and varied staff was being assembled to assist
Tycho in his efforts. In addition to Tycho Jr. and Franz
Tengnagel, there was Christian Severin Longomontanus, a
talented Danish astronomer who had spent his entire career
working for Tycho. Johannes Müller, mathematician to the
elector of Brandenburg, and his family arrived the following
month, pushing Kepler further down in the hierarchy. With
Tycho's common-law wife, Kirsten Jørgensdatter, their
other children, various other assistants, and servants, the
small castle was crowded.

Kepler was rather bewildered by the scene and felt lost
amid Tycho's large household. Nor was their collaboration
what he had hoped for. He came to use Tycho's superior
observational data to test and develop his polyhedral cosmo-

text continues on page 49

In 1575, the king of Denmark granted Tycho Brahe the Island of Hven in the Øresund (the strait between present-day Denmark and Sweden) along with enough money to build and run an observatory. During the next twenty years, Tycho made Uraniborg, "the castle of Urania," into Europe's first scientific research institute. Starting in 1576, he had a Renaissance castle custom-built there to correspond to his needs. Its main feature was two second-story observing decks where instruments were permanently installed under removable conical roofs. There was also a library, where Tycho had a huge brass globe five feet in diameter, on which the positions of stars were patiently engraved when they were known with sufficient accuracy. In the basement, there were 16 furnaces of different kinds for alchemical experiments. Eight small rooms under the roof gables on the third floor housed assistants and students.

Tycho had instrument shops, where he was constantly producing more refined and accurate instruments, and a printing press, so he could publish his findings. In the watchtower of his castle wall, he even had a jail. Elsewhere on the island, he built his own paper mill and fishponds. Later on, Tycho decided that it would be better to have a separate observatory, where larger instruments could be installed down out of the wind. This subterranean observatory, called Stjerneborg, "the castle of the stars," housed Tycho's largest and most sophisticated instruments.

text continued from page 65

logical hypothesis from the *Mysterium cosmographicum*. But he found Tycho to be secretive with his data. For his part, Tycho was not about to give his data away, and he did not particularly trust Kepler, especially given his suspicious connection with Ursus.

Tycho was at the stage in his career when he needed to spend time analyzing his many years of observations to distill accurate planetary theories from the raw data. For this, he needed many assistants to do the calculations. Tycho assigned Kepler to work under Longomontanus's supervision on the theory of Mars. The situation was galling to Kepler. He found himself lost in the commotion at Benatky, picking up dribs and drabs of greatly-desired information as Tycho casually let fall a reference to the location of a planet's apogee (its furthest distance from the earth) or node (where its orbit intersected the sun's orbit) as he held court during dinner in the crowded second floor dining room.

Even though Kepler could not get on with the development of the polyhedral hypothesis, for which he needed data on all of the planets, there was still work he could do on his planet-moving force hypothesis, for which he could use just the Mars observations. And within a few months he had come up with some remarkable confirmation. If the planets were really moved by a force coming from the sun, then the geometry of the planets' theories should reflect that. First, he found that, no matter what he tried, Mars's orbit had to take into account the sun's actual position, which made sense if it was the source of motion. Second, and more importantly, by ingeniously manipulating the observations of Mars, Kepler was able to investigate the earth's orbit, and he found that the earth shared the physically non-uniform motion of the other planets; it too speeded up when it approached the sun and slowed down as it receded. Astronomers had never previously understood that the theory of the earth was so similar to the theories of other planets. In fact, in the *Mysterium cosmographicum*,

Kepler had had to acknowledge that the planet-moving force hypothesis did not work with the earth's orbit. Now, suddenly, the earth's motion confirmed the planet-moving force hypothesis. Though the result was immensely gratifying to Kepler, Tycho Brahe, like Maestlin, objected vehemently to his use of physical analysis in the derivation of planetary theory.

The first summer of Kepler's collaboration with Tycho Brahe was also marred by some friction between the two astronomers over Kepler's status and professional prospects. Facing the extreme uncertainty of how events would unfold in Styria, Kepler pressured Tycho for a formal position and contract. To Tycho, Kepler's demands were an affront. He had problems of his own collecting his salary from the emperor and pushing on with the renovation of Benatky. However, he was working behind the scenes to secure an imperial salary for Kepler, by having the emperor officially summon Kepler to assist Tycho Brahe for two years in his astronomical work. During this time, Kepler would continue to receive his 200 florin salary as district mathematician in Styria, and the emperor would supplement it with another 100 florins. Since the request to release Kepler for this assignment would come from the emperor, it was believed the representatives of the Estates of Styria would not be able to turn it down.

With his future prospects looking much better, Kepler prepared to return home in May. As a final gesture of goodwill, Tycho arranged for Kepler to travel with his third cousin, Frederick Rosenkrantz, as far as Vienna. They departed on June 1. Rosenkrantz would have had tales to tell as they traveled southeast through Bohemia into Austria. Like his cousin, Rosenkrantz was a Danish nobleman whose relations with his native land were strained. He had fled Denmark after getting a young lady-in-waiting pregnant, but had been captured and sentenced to the loss of two fingers and his nobility. But then, the sentence had been commuted to service in the Christian campaign against the

Islamic Turks, who had advanced through the Balkans and were threatening Austria's southern border. After stopping to visit his cousin at Benatky, he was traveling to Vienna to join the Austrian troops. Unbeknownst to him, Rosenkrantz was already being immortalized in a way. In 1592, when on a diplomatic mission to England with another cousin of Tycho's, Knud Gyldenstierne, he had made an impression on the young playwright William Shakespeare and had earned himself a bit part in *Hamlet*.

The hopeful joy that attended the preliminary results of

In this mural, printed in Tycho's Mechanica, Tycho points to the heavens. A cutaway image of Uraniborg shows the observing decks, the library with the great celestial globe, and the alchemical furnaces in the basement.

his research on Mars and the prospect of returning to Prague to continue his work with Tycho Brahe quickly dissipated upon Kepler's return to Graz. The Styrian councilors were not well disposed toward releasing Kepler to return to Prague. Kepler's astronomical speculations were out of place in the uneasy atmosphere that gripped Styria. It would be better, they concluded, if Kepler were to turn his attention to something useful, like going to Italy to study medicine and then returning to practice as a physician.

That summer, Kepler tried to interest Archduke Ferdinand to hire him as his personal mathematician, as his cousin the emperor had done with Tycho Brahe, but Ferdinand had other plans. On July 27, 1600, a notice appeared: an ecclesiastical commission was coming to Graz. At 6 A.M. on July 31, all citizens would present themselves for an examination of their faith. Anyone who was not Catholic or did not pledge to convert to Catholicism would be expelled from the country. Archduke Ferdinand himself accompanied the commissioners. They set up a large table in the middle of the church. During the course of three days, one by one, more than a thousand people approached the table and declared themselves. When Kepler's turn came, he declared himself a Lutheran and unwilling to convert. His name was inscribed on the list of banished men, 15th of 61. He was given six weeks and three days to be out of the country.

Kepler began to make preparations to leave. He only had to figure out where to go. The arrangement with Tycho Brahe was ruined, for it presupposed his receiving the greater part of his pay from Styria. Desperately, he wrote to Maestlin, again asking whether some "little professorship" might be found for him at Tübingen. Not hearing from Maestlin and having no other options, he would head back to Prague. He had been advised that Tycho would find a way to take care of him, and, indeed, Tycho responded to his distress by writing that the collapse of their arrangement did not matter; Kepler should not hesitate but should return with confidence.

On September 30, 1600, two weeks beyond the expulsion deadline, Kepler left Graz with his wife and daughter and two wagons containing all their possessions. His stay in Graz was over.

Kepler had grave misgivings about returning to Tycho's service. He was too proud and insecure to depend entirely on Tycho's mercy, but there was nowhere else to go. Underway, he was struck with a terrible fever. When he arrived in Prague on October 19, Baron Hoffmann took him in, a sick, exhausted, and depressed man. When Maestlin finally reported that there was no prospect of a job for him in Tübingen, Kepler was shattered. He replied with pathetic resignation, "I cannot describe what paroxysm of melancholy your letter caused me . . . For here in Prague I have found everything uncertain, even my life. The only certainty is staying here until I get well or die." A serious cough joined the fever, and Kepler feared he had tuberculosis. His wife became ill as well.

When he was finally well enough to go to work, he found Tycho's circumstances substantially changed as well. Tycho had abandoned his unfinished "New Uraniborg" at Benatky for cramped quarters in the city. When the plague that had gripped Prague the previous year had receded, Emperor Rudolf II and his court had returned, and the emperor desired the presence of his astrologer, Tycho Brahe. It was precisely the kind of work Tycho disliked—it was difficult to convince the emperor of the limit of astrological prognostications—but it was essential to satisfy his patron. He had packed up the instruments and was doing his best to accommodate them at his new home in the city. Kepler and his family were also squeezed in somewhere when they left Baron Hoffmann's. Tycho's personnel had also changed. Longomontanus had left him after many years of service and returned to Denmark to make a career for himself independent of Tycho. None of the various Germans Tycho had tried to attract, including Johannes Müller, had worked out either.

Kepler's fever raged on intermittently for months through the spring of 1601, and he was unable to work much on his Mars research. His fever subsided only that summer, during a visit back to Styria. Old Jobst Müller had died, and Kepler went back to look after his wife's inheritance, hoping to convert her assets into cash. His effort was fruitless, but after he returned from his four month visit around the end of August, he felt really well and rested. When he returned to Prague, Tycho had a scheme to secure for him a formal imperial appointment. The fact of the matter was, Kepler was about the only assistant Tycho had left. Longomontanus was gone. Tengnagel had married Tycho's daughter Elizabeth that summer and gone off to Deventer, Holland, taking another assistant, Johannes Erikson, with him.

Putting a great deal of faith in Kepler, Tycho took him to court and introduced him to the emperor, a strange, shy man with round childlike eyes set in a face anchored by a prominent chin, the characteristic feature of the Hapsburg family. Tycho presented a plan to compile a great set of astronomical tables and asked permission to name them *The Rudolfine Tables*, after the emperor. It was a grand gesture.

Tycho worked as astrologer to Holy Roman Emperor Rudolf II (below) and proposed a great set of astronomical tables that were named the Rudolfine Tables *in his honor.*

The great astronomical tables, like the *Alphonsine* (Ptolemaic) or the *Prutenic* (Copernican), had been named after their sponsors, ensuring them a kind of immortality. If Tycho's lived up to their promise, they would be a magnificent monument indeed. Rudolf liked the idea very much. The only thing Tycho would require would be a salary for his assistant, Johannes Kepler.

The paperwork for Kepler's salary does not seem even to have been put in motion when it became obsolete. Ever since moving into the city, Tycho's social circle had expanded, and without much observing being done at night, he got back into the noble pastime of attending parties where a great deal of hard drinking was done. On October 13, 1601, he attended a party at the house of Peter Vok Rozmberk. In order to avoid some breach of etiquette, Tycho remained seated at the table for far longer than his bladder allowed. It was a fatal miscalculation. By the time he got home, he could no longer urinate, and it quickly became clear that he was in serious trouble. It is impossible to know precisely what afflicted Tycho. Passing even a little urine was excruciatingly painful, and as the wastes built up in his body, he suffered from what Kepler called "intestinal fever," probably what we now call uremia. He passed sleepless nights in agony. Knowing that he would die, he spoke to Kepler, and begged him to present his research in the Tychonic system of the world rather than the Copernican. Then he became delirious, repeating over and over, "Let me not be seen to have lived in vain." Finally, as Kepler inscribed on the final page of Tycho's observation log,

> On October 24, 1601, when his delirium had subsided for a few hours, amid the prayers, tears, and efforts of his family to console him, his strength failed and he passed away very peacefully.
>
> At this time, then, his series of celestial observations was interrupted, and the observations of thirty-eight years came to an end.

On November 4, draped in black cloth and decorated in gold with the Brahe coat of arms, Tycho's casket was carried by twelve imperial officers, all of them noblemen, in a procession to the Protestant Tyne Cathedral. Accompanying it were black banners carrying lists of his titles and accomplishments in gold letters. His riderless horse and men carrying his arms and armor followed behind. Then followed a parade of people: noblemen, barons, ambassadors, his assistants, including Kepler, Tycho's family, and distinguished citizens. A solid wall of humanity lined the route as the procession snaked through the city. And in the church, there was scarcely any room to be found. Tycho was interred in the nave, his grave marked by a magnificent red marble frieze depicting him in full armor. He rests there still.

Kepler had scarcely any time to ponder his future. Within two days, he was informed the he would become the emperor's new mathematician, with responsibility to care for Tycho's instruments and to complete Tycho's unfinished publications, the most important of which would be the *Rudolfine Tables*. At the time of his appointment, Kepler was the obvious choice. There was no other qualified candidate around, and only weeks earlier Tycho had presented him as his primary collaborator in the *Rudolfine Tables*. Still, the emperor recognized that Tycho's instruments and observing logs rightly belonged to his heirs, so he simply bought them for the extraordinary sum of 20,000 florins—an amount sufficient to pay Kepler's previous salary in Styria for a century

Tycho's renowned instruments include the Great Equitorial Armillary (left) and the Trigonal Sextant (right). After Tycho's death, Emperor Rudolf II bought these instruments and made Kepler responsible for looking after them.

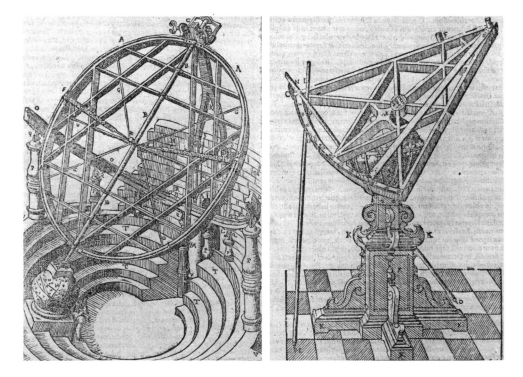

or to buy a half dozen country estates in Bohemia. However, money at the court of Rudolf II had an unearthly quality. The emperor promised whatever he wanted; collecting it from the imperial treasury was another matter. Kepler consistently had problems collecting even his 500 florin annual salary.

The terms of Kepler's succession to Tycho's position sowed the seeds for a conflict with Tycho Brahe's heirs that would exercise a significant influence on the form of Kepler's future scientific work. When Tengnagel returned from England the following summer, he discovered that the heirs had hardly received any money from the treasury. Tengnagel was a nobleman, and Tycho's son-in-law by virtue of his marriage to Elizabeth, so he represented the family's interests. First, he thought he could exert some pressure by suing to get the observing logs back until they were paid for. But then it occurred to him that there was money in the *Rudolfine Tables* project. In October 1602, he managed to get responsibility for the *Rudolfine Tables* transferred to himself, at double Kepler's salary. To add insult to injury, he accused Kepler of sloth and saw to it that someone was assigned to check up on what Kepler was doing.

At this point, the emperor had two mathematicians, and he may well have wondered what he was paying Kepler to do. Kepler was compelled to name the books he would compose to justify his continuing employment. It was a fateful moment, for in grasping among his half-finished projects Kepler named what would be two of the most significant books of seventeenth-century science. As he described the situation in a letter to a friend,

> . . . because I have had my diligence called into doubt, I have assumed the obligation for two works. The one to be ready for Easter 1603 will be Commentaries on the Theory of Mars (or whatever else the name might be), or The Key to a Universal Astronomy . . . The other, to be completed within 8 weeks, will be the Astronomiae pars optica [The Optical Part of Astronomy].

The *Astronomiae pars optica*, whose full title ended up being *Ad Vitellionem paralipomena, quibus astronomiae pars optica traditur* (Supplements to Witelo, in which the Astronomical Part of Astronomy is Treated), had its origin in an essay Kepler had composed in the summer of 1600 on the formation of pinhole images. Earlier that year, Tycho had told him about his observations of a partial solar eclipse, in which the moon passed in front of the sun without completely covering it. Tycho had observed the event without looking directly at the sun by allowing sunlight to fall through a pinhole onto a white screen, where it formed an image of the eclipsed sun. Using his measurements, Tycho concluded that total solar eclipses, in which the moon would completely cover the sun, were impossible. Kepler was skeptical regarding this claim, for there were ample accounts of total solar eclipses in the historic record. After observing a partial solar eclipse for himself from Graz on July 10, 1600, Kepler had carefully analyzed the formation of pinhole images and come to the correct conclusion that their accuracy depended on the size of the aperture. This finding explained Tycho's incorrect conclusion about the possibility of solar eclipses; his pinhole image of the sun was distorted by the size of the aperture and slightly too large, which had led Tycho to believe the moon could never totally cover it. Kepler's essay was a nice little supplement, as he put it, to Witelo's *Optics*, the standard 13th-century treatise on optical theory.

Kepler's essay had clear implications for astronomical observations, and two years later, he grasped for it as something that he could easily get ready for publication within a few weeks. But here, Kepler's legendary inability to focus on one problem at a time got the better of him. First, he wanted to add the other elements of optics that were relevant to astronomy, such as atmospheric refraction. And then he got the work tangled up with a comprehensive treatise on eclipses and the sizes and distances of the sun and moon that he had also been working on. Ultimately, he decided that he could not really write on astronomical observation without taking into account the function of the human eye.

He managed to disentangle the treatise on the sizes and distances of the sun and moon and put it aside, but the material on the function of the eye was a great success. In addition to pinhole images, he was able to publish the first correct account of vision and the eye. For centuries, how we see, a complicated question involving the nature of light, geometrical optics, and the anatomy of the eye, had been a topic of investigation by natural philosophers and optical theorists. By rigorously building on his other optical analyses, Kepler realized that, rather than rays of light being "captured" somehow in the fluid of the eyeball, the lens in the eye *projects* the image of the outside world onto the surface of the retina. Kepler's optical principles dictated that such an image is formed upside down and backwards on the retina; how that image is taken into the mind and rectified to be right side up and frontwards, he could not say. With the help of his new account of vision, he was able to add to this a precise description of the function of different eyeglasses in the correction of nearsightedness and farsightedness. Finally, in the introductory chapter on the nature of light, he was able to deduce the correct relationship for the intensity of light as a function of its distance from the source. Reasoning that light spreads out from a point in a sphere, he concluded that its intensity should be proportional to the area of that sphere, or the intensity should be inversely proportional to the square of the distance.

Some of the problems Kepler attacked did not yield, such as a precise account of the theory of refraction, the bending of light rays as they pass from one medium to another. Nevertheless, starting from an analysis of a limited problem in Witelo's *Optics*, he ended up with such a thorough reworking of optical theory that his *The Optical Part of Astronomy* became the foundation work of seventeenth-century optical theory. It was not a bad performance for some-

Kepler's theory of retinal vision as depicted in René Descartes's Dioptrique. The triangle (V) is projected onto the retina at R and the circle (Y) at T. Thus the image of the outside world is projected upside down and backwards onto the retina.

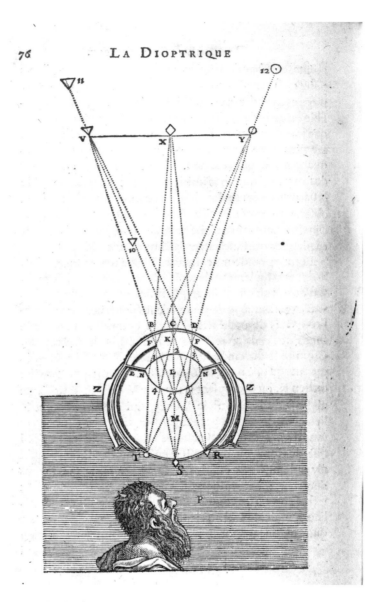

one who had to "justify his employment."

Kepler had originally promised the *Astronomiae pars optica* in time for Christmas 1602. As it swelled to become a tome of 450 pages, publication was delayed, and he did not finally present the finished manuscript to the emperor until January 1604. It was printed in Frankfurt, and appeared in time for the great Frankfurt book fair in the fall of 1604.

When the book was out of his hands, Kepler turned his attention to the other project he had promised the emperor, a work he referred to as *The Commentaries on Mars*, or *The Key to a Universal Astronomy*. It was an odd genre for an astronomical book; a single planet's motion had never before been the subject of a book-length treatment. This tight focus was in some sense contrived, because Tengnagel had snatched away responsibility for the larger project of coming up with tables for all of the planets. But Kepler realized that it would be a work of great significance, for it was by using observations of Mars that he had discovered that a major change was needed in the theory of the earth's orbit. He recognized the significance of this finding even before committing to the *Commentaries*, writing in a letter, "In short, I have beheld the sun in the theory of Mars as though in a mirror, in that I see how and to what extent it affects all planets. I take from Mars the example for treating the others. And thus I hope presently for all the best for every part of astronomy."

So far, Kepler's work on Mars had vindicated his novel, physical approach to deriving the orbits of the planets. He had had the hunch, based upon his notion of a planet-moving force coming forth from the sun, that the earth's orbit had to be like the other planets, so that it would move faster when it was closer to the sun and slower when it was further away. And he had been right. If he could demonstrate that his "celestial physics" was valid, he would be able to argue that only the Copernican system of the universe made physical sense and that it was true. Since, as he believed, the heliocentric system was a material symbol of God in His creation, establishing its truth continued to have an important religious dimension as well.

Since Tycho's death, Kepler's Mars research had taken a turn toward becoming ever more physical. He had started with the planet-moving force hypothesis put forward in the *Mysterium cosmographicum*, but he had realized that his formulation was flawed. He had then begun using the simple principle that a planet's speed around the sun was inversely proportional to its distance: the closer it is, the faster it goes around. But how could one describe the ensuing motion mathematically? It was a difficult question, because on an eccentric orbit the planet would be slightly changing its distance, and therefore its speed, all the way around. A modern mathematician would use calculus to calculate the effect, but it had not been invented yet.

Kepler first took a brute-force approach. He calculated the distance from the sun to Mars at each and every degree around an eccentric circular orbit and used the sum of those distances as a measure of the time it took to get from one place to another. It was a tedious and unsatisfactory experience, but as he was thinking about it, he remembered that Archimedes, the Greek mathematician who lived at the turn of the second century B.C., had used a similar trick with sums of distances to calculate the area of a circle. Surely, the area swept out by Mars as it went around its orbit would be a good measurement of the sum of the distances. In this way, Kepler came to the approximating principle that the area swept out by a planet as it goes around its orbit will be equal in equal time intervals. This later came to be known, through an historical accident, as Kepler's "second law" of planetary motion, even though he came upon it first.

He tried applying his new area law on a circular orbit that was slightly eccentric, so that the sun was located off center along an axis that passed through the center of the circle and defined Mars's closest and furthest positions from the sun. When he did so, he realized that, in his calculated position, Mars was spending too much time along the sides of its orbit away from the axis. It would have to be speeded up there, which meant that the orbit would have to be squeezed in a little along the sides to redistribute that area, or time, into other parts of the orbit. As he put it, it was as though you held a fat-bellied sausage and squeezed it in the

KEPLER'S FIRST TWO LAWS

K epler's first two laws are:

1. The planets move in elliptical orbits, with the sun at one focus.

2. The line connecting the planet and the sun sweeps out equal areas in equal times.

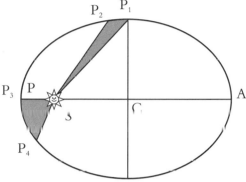

The two laws are illustrated in the figure above, which shows the elliptical orbit of a planet, with the sun at the focus marked S. The size of an ellipse is usually given in terms of the *semimajor axis*, which is half the long axis PA, or the distance PC. And the eccentricity is defined as the ratio of the distance of the sun from the center to the size of the semimajor axis, or $e = \frac{SC}{PC}$. The ellipse depicted above has an extraordinarily large eccentricity compared to the orbits of the planets, which would look like perfect circles if shown at this scale.

Kepler's second law states the area swept out by the planet as it moves along its orbit from position P_1 to P_2 (the shaded area P_1SP_2) must be the same as the area swept out in an equal time interval as it moves from P_3 to P_4 (area P_3SP_4). As is apparent in the diagram, this means that when a planet's distance to the sun is smaller, it must move correspondingly further around its orbit in the same time interval. Consequently, the planet moves most quickly around perihelion (P) and most slowly around aphelion (A), or as Kepler would have expressed it, it moves most quickly when it is near the source of the planet-moving force and most slowly when it is furthest away.

middle, forcing the meat out into the ends. Thus, by exercising his physical intuition, Kepler came to the conclusion that the orbit must be some kind of oval, rather than a perfect circle. The rest of his effort would be devoted to determining which oval, in conjunction with his area law, produced positions that agreed with Tycho's exquisitely accurate observations.

The task of determining exactly which oval was appropriate and how to generate it was a torturously complex process that took all of 1604. Kepler wrote to Longomontanus that he had tried it twenty different ways. Eventually, he resorted to using an ellipse as an approximation of a likely oval orbit. Ellipses are a subset of ovals that have mathematical properties that make them much easier to use, especially when calculating areas. With this approximating elliptical orbit and the area law, the error was almost precisely opposite what it had been with a circular orbit. The sausage had been squeezed too much. He then concluded that the correct orbit must lie somewhere in between.

This new in-between ellipse had the interesting feature that the sun precisely occupied one of its foci. Indeed, Kepler's interest in this new orbit had originally been spurred by considering exactly how far in from a circle Mars had come at the point one quarter of the way around its orbit. He knew that it should come in about half as far as his previous attempt, and then suddenly realized that, measured from the sun, there was a concise trigonometrical way to describe that distance, and it entailed an elliptical orbit. Moreover, he understood precisely how Mars's distance from the sun changed throughout its orbit, and this particular ellipse resolved a nagging problem about the accuracy of his area law approximation. This flood of considerations came to him at once. It was, he wrote, "as if I were roused from a dream and saw a new light." Thus, he came to his "first law" of planetary motion, that the orbits of the planets are ellipses with the sun at one focus.

The book was not supposed to be merely about a new theory for Mars. It was the debut of a whole new physical approach to astronomical theory, which happened to be based on Kepler's Mars research. Therefore he entitled it *Astronomia nova AITIOLOGHTOΣ, seu physica coelestis, tradita commentariis de motibus stellae Martis*, that is, A New Astronomy Based upon Causes, or Celestial Physics, Treated by Means of Commentaries on the Motions of Mars. He knew it could not *prove* that his physical astronomy or the Copernican system was true. Mathematical astronomers would be all too willing to disregard what he thought would be the most compelling feature of the book, the physical basis of his new astronomical theories. His journey through astronomical theory carries the weight of his argument. "No other approach," he wrote, "would succeed than that founded upon the very physical causes of the motions." In the end, the argument is rhetorical: the fact that Kepler discovered the ellipse and the area law following certain hunches does not logically establish that his reasoning is correct.

Around Easter 1605, Kepler realized that Mars's orbit was an ellipse, but he still had much more to write. Before Kepler could publish he also had to settle with Tengnagel, who had the right to approve any of Kepler's work based on Tycho's observations. The prospect of having Tengnagel meddling in his work was almost more than Kepler could bear, especially since Tengnagel had essentially abandoned his work on the *Rudolfine Tables*. Kepler agreed to let Tengnagel write a preface to his book, in which Tengnagel admonished the reader "not to be swayed by anything of Kepler's, especially his liberty in disagreeing with Brahe in physical arguments."

Everything went slowly, and it was not until 1609 that the *Astronomia nova* finally appeared. The emperor had reserved the right to distribute every copy of his personal mathematician's work, but in the end Kepler had to turn the entire edition over to the printer to cover unpaid costs. It was not a very auspicious launching for what would turn out to be one of the most important astronomical works in history.

The *Astronomia nova* was a tall, handsome—if slightly austere—volume of some 340 pages. It is considered to be Kepler's masterpiece. It is a work of great mathematical genius and breathtaking inventiveness. His contentious point that knowledge of the planet's motions can only be determined by consideration of the physical cause of those motions eventually came to be recognized as true. It is interesting, however, that, though he showed that astronomy should be physical, his particular physics was ultimately discarded. In the generations after his death, it came to be recognized that there is no force coming from the sun that pushes the planets around. The celestial mechanics that Isaac Newton developed is entirely different. The planets' tendency is to continue moving in straight lines, and the gravitational attraction of the sun pulling them in constrains them to move around it. But even with this different physics, Kepler's first two laws necessarily follow: the orbits of the planets are elliptical with the sun at one focus and the area swept out by a planet is equal in equal times.

The great work of the *Astronomia nova* now completed, Kepler took a break from his studies, and his mind turned to Galileo. How would the Italian, who also sought physical proofs of Copernicus's system, react to Kepler's painstaking presentation of his physical astronomy? Little did he know that Galileo was not studying the *Astronomia nova* but making the astronomical discoveries that would make him the talk of Europe and secure his reputation for all time.

On March 15, 1610, the startling news came to Prague that Galileo had discovered four new planets. Kepler's friend the imperial councilor Johann Matthäus Wackher von Wackenfels was so excited by the report that he stopped his carriage at Kepler's house and called him down to the street to tell him. The two were so overcome that they could scarcely talk. They babbled and laughed in excitement at the news. Kepler was excited but ashamed and confused as well. What did the discovery mean for his polyhedral hypothesis? He had already determined the necessary number of planets, and there was room for no more.

Galileo's book had not even left the press when the news first flew to Prague. The first copy of his *Sidereus nuncius* (The Starry Messenger) (1610) to reach the city belonged to the curious emperor, who lent it to his mathematician for his opinion. Kepler was immediately relieved. The new planets were previously-unknown satellites of Jupiter, discovered by Galileo using the newly invented telescope. In addition to Jupiter's moons, Galileo demonstrated definitively that the surface of the moon was rough and earthlike. He also turned his telescope to the stars, revealing thousands that had previously remained unseen. The Milky Way he resolved into a myriad of stars whose faint light combined into the nebulous streak across the sky.

The advent of telescopic observation would open a new era for astronomy. In the meantime, Galileo's announce-

These images from Galileo's Sidereus nuncius *depict the surface of the moon as viewed through the telescope. Galileo's observations showed that the moon was mountainous and earthlike.*

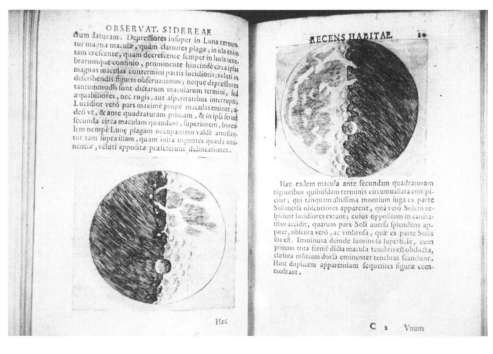

ment was so radical that many could scarcely believe it. Because Kepler was imperial mathematician, his opinion would carry some weight and lend Galileo important credibility. Galileo sent a copy of his book along with a letter asking for Kepler's judgment to the Tuscan ambassador in Prague, who had the book delivered to Kepler. On April 13, Kepler visited the ambassador's residence, where Galileo's request was read to him. An official courier was returning to Tuscany within a week, and Kepler promised his reply would be ready for the return trip. He finished his letter to Galileo on April 19.

So many other people were anxious to know what Kepler had said that he had the letter printed as a small 35-page book with the title *Dissertatio cum nunceo sidereo* (A Conversation with the Starry Messenger) (1610). It was an unusual work. Kepler did not have a telescope, so he could not confirm the observations. (Try as he might he could not get Galileo to send him one and eventually had to borrow one to see the new phenomena for himself.) In the meantime, the most Kepler could do to lend Galileo support was establish the plausibility of what Galileo had reported, beginning with the telescope itself. In some ways the principle of magnifying images using a combination of lenses had been alluded to in previous optical theory. But it was something Kepler had missed in his *Astronomia pars optica*. Five months later, he had cracked the problem and the next year Kepler published the first detailed optical theory of two lens systems in his *Dioptrice* (1611), including a superior telescope design using two convex lenses, now called the "astronomical" or "Keplerian" telescope.

Otherwise, Kepler could only respond enthusiastically to Galileo's discoveries and speculate about their meaning. With regard to Galileo's account of lunar geography, Kepler admitted that he was totally convinced by Galileo's observations and analysis of mountains and craters on the moon, and he speculated that the cratered appearance was due perhaps to the moon being light and porous (which according to Kepler's physical astronomy would explain its rapid revolution around the earth). Or perhaps the craters were great circular ramparts built by lunar inhabitants, in whose shade they could shelter during the inhospitable 14 days of continuous sunlight on the moon's surface.

Jupiter's moons were by far the most spectacular of Galileo's discoveries. For Kepler, they were significant because they had implications in favor of heliocentrism. First, the fact that Jupiter also had moons seemed to remove the objection that the earth could not travel around the sun without losing its moon. Also, the fact that the moons revolved in the plane of Jupiter's rotation implied that the moons were being swept around by a planet-moving force coming from Jupiter, just as Kepler had suggested in the *Astronomia nova* that the moon is moved by the earth's rotation. Finally, Jupiter's moons suggested to Kepler that Jupiter must be inhabited by intelligent beings. Why else would God have endowed Jupiter with this feature we cannot see?

With the publication of the *Dissertatio,* Kepler became the first astronomer to come out publicly in favor of Galileo and his discoveries. The support of the imperial mathematician helped to subdue the sniping Galileo faced from his critics. Yet, in return, Kepler received from Galileo scarcely a word of thanks and no acknowledgment of Kepler's more substantial achievements in astronomy. Though Kepler tried a few more times to engage the Italian in correspondence, apart from one inconsequential note some 17 years later, he never heard from Galileo again. Though two of the greatest astronomers in history lived at the same time, and even communicated, there was barely a connection between them. In his unassuming way, Kepler never complained of Galileo's offensive disregard. And Galileo apparently took little notice of Kepler's reform of astronomical theory.

It was now 1611; Kepler was 39 years old. In the 11 years since coming to Prague, Johannes Kepler had grown from an insecure refugee into a leading figure in the imperial capital's learned circles and a man of international scientific reputation. His status as scientific heir to Tycho Brahe and the flow of important works that issued from his pen lent him an air of astronomical omniscience that the English poet John Donne described in his satire *Ignatius his Conclave* (1611), where he wrote that "ever since Tycho Brahe's death [Kepler] hath received it into his care, that no new thing should be done in heaven without his knowledge."

The same period that saw Kepler's rise to fame saw the decline of his eccentric patron into madness. Observing the emperor's governance from afar before moving to Prague, Kepler had marveled at the emperor's "Archimedian manner," a kind of dynamic immobility, as he saw it, in which the emperor nonetheless managed to maintain a long, stalemated war against the Ottoman Turks and, at the same time, kept the empire's fractious states from disintegrating. But since Kepler's arrival in Prague in 1600, the emperor's pathological shyness and extreme stubbornness had given way to isolation, paralyzing indecision, and paranoia. Turning away from the world, he became a recluse, shut in among his precious collections in Hradschin, a virtual prisoner in his own castle. It was widely reported that his erratic mental state had deteriorated into insanity.

As Rudolf's intransigence and inactivity began to imperil the house of Hapsburg and the empire, a conspiracy was hatched against him. At a secret meeting of the Austrian Hapsburgs in Vienna in April 1606, the family agreed to recognize Rudolf's estranged, ambitious younger brother Matthias as head of the family. Two years later, Matthias moved against his brother under force of arms, leading an army of 20,000 men from Vienna, through Moravia, into Bohemia, and to within a day's march of Prague. Facing certain defeat, the emperor capitulated. He ceded Matthias the kingdom of Hungary and archduchies of Austria and Moravia effective immediately, retaining only Bohemia,

Silesia, and Lusatia to himself, though Rudolf had to ensure Matthias's succession as king of Bohemia after his death.

The weakened emperor now faced pressure from the powerful Protestant representatives of the Bohemian Estates, the representative assembly in Bohemia, who exacted from him a Letter of Majesty (1609) guaranteeing freedom of religion. Chaffing under the concessions they had extorted and descending into insanity, Rudolf made a desperate bid to regain control of his country and its capital. The following winter, Rudolf inexplicably invited his cousin, Archduke Leopold V, bishop of Passua, to invade Bohemia. Leopold's army pillaged its way through Bohemia to Prague, invading and looting the Hradcany and the Lesser Town.

A spirited defense by Protestant troops (who for their part also looted Catholic churches and monasteries in the Old Town) and a large bribe put an end to Leopold's attack, but Rudolf was finished. In the midst of the crisis, the Protestant representatives sided with Matthias. Rudolf was deposed, and on May 23, 1611, Matthias was crowned king of Bohemia. Deranged and powerless, the emperor lived out his days in the Hradschin, where he died within a year on January 20, 1612.

Kepler stayed loyal to his patron to the end. Though he was consulted for advice, he did his best to keep astrology out of the gullible emperor's troubled mind. And when the emperor's enemies approached Kepler, he spun the astrological analysis in the emperor's favor, predicting long life for him and trouble for Matthias. Still, Kepler could see that the situation was deteriorating. He took care to have backup plans ready and found a promising situation in the Upper Austrian capital of Linz. After the emperor's death, nothing held Kepler in Prague, and in the middle of April he left the city for Linz.

A portrait by Hans von Aachen, probably of Kepler, from around 1612.

The Harmony of the World

When Kepler arrived in Linz in May 1612, he was emotionally exhausted. The splendid intellectual society in the imperial capital in which he had been intensely creative and productive had submerged into civil war. The horrible events of the previous year had robbed him of the will to continue his astronomical studies.

The year 1611 had been devastating and sorrowful, not only for Prague but also for Kepler's family. As the year opened, his wife Barbara was sick with Hungarian fever and showed signs of a mental disorder. As she was recovering, all three children were struck with smallpox. Eight-year-old Susanna (his second daughter with that name) and three-year-old Ludwig survived, but Kepler's favorite, darling six-year-old Friedrich, died on February 19, and Barbara sank into a depression. Then, Archduke Leopold's troops invaded, and Kepler's neighborhood in Old Town was overrun by unruly Bohemian peasants loosely organized for the Protestant cause. At this point, Kepler redoubled his efforts to move his family away from Prague. But even as he was returning from a trip to Linz to make arrangements in June 1611, he found Barbara deathly ill from a contagious fever brought into Prague by Matthias's Austrian troops. She died on July 3, 1611.

Though he was glad to be away from the charged and uncertain atmosphere in Prague, his arrival in quiet Linz was accompanied by pangs of guilt. Three years before, he had begun planning the move to accommodate his wife, whose simple nature had never been at ease in the imperial capital. He had chosen the place because of its similarity to Barbara's native Graz. Linz was the provincial capital of Upper Austria, the duchy northeast of Styria. Like its neighbor before Archduke Ferdinand's confessional cleansing, Upper Austria was predominantly Protestant. Yet it was within the Hapsburgs' hereditary lands, so Kepler was able to arrange to continue his work there. Now, without his wife, the imperial mathematician felt out of place in a city that did not boast a university or printing press and whose Protestant school was inferior even to Graz's.

Finding a position for a man of Kepler's stature had been ticklish. At the invitation of some Upper Austrian lords, Kepler had tendered his services to the representatives of the Estates of Upper Austria after Rudolf's abdication. A contract was drawn up according to which Kepler would continue work on the *Rudolfine Tables*, compose a map of Upper Austria, and produce whatever mathematical, philosophical, or historical studies were "useful and suitable." In practice, he had the same job he had had in Graz: district mathematician and teacher in the district school. It was a rather ordinary position for the man he had become, but the authorities in Linz paid him his 400 florins regularly, which was far more than he could say for his exalted imperial appointment.

Kepler's high profile unfortunately exposed him to unwelcome scrutiny from his coreligionists in Linz. Immediately upon his arrival, Kepler sought communion from the chief pastor, Daniel Hitzler, himself an alumnus of the Tübingen theological seminary. Since his seminary days, Kepler's questioning of Lutheran dogma had grown into a refusal to sign the Formula of Concord, the Lutherans' strict charter of belief. The issue that particularly concerned him was the interpretation of the Eucharist, in which Kepler sided with the Lutherans' hated rivals, the Calvinists. Hitzler required Kepler to sign the Formula of Concord. Kepler declined to subscribe to the relevant clause regarding the interpretation of the Eucharist and Hitzler denied him communion, thereby excluding him from the congregation.

That his strongly held personal convictions should exclude him from the Protestant community was intensely painful to Kepler, especially since it was on a fine point of dogma only theologians could appreciate. In August, he appealed Hitzler's ruling to the church consistory in Stuttgart. His petition was swiftly rejected in a shaming letter that upheld Hitzler on all points and advised Kepler to refrain from "theological speculations" and concern himself with his mathematical studies. As a "lost little sheep" he should obediently follow the voice of the arch-shepherd. Although Kepler was incapable of being "sheepish" about matters of conscience, he promised to be quiet and make no trouble.

Nevertheless, he became the object of rampant gossip about his unorthodox views. Unlike those who sought to police belief and vilify their opponents, Kepler drew elements of religious truth from Lutheranism, Calvinism, and Catholicism. He was alternately accused of being fickle and wanting to found his own unique Keplerian creed. He responded bitterly, "It makes me heartsick that the three big factions have so miserably torn up the truth among themselves that I have to gather the little scraps together wherever I find them." Even as the German-speaking lands were inching inexorably toward a devastating religious war, he never ceased to try to act as a conciliator among the faiths. He was repaid with suspicion, backbiting, and threats. The final chapter of Kepler's exclusion from communion came in the wake of a painful and awkward visit to his old theology professor Matthias Hafenreffer in Tübingen in the fall of

1617. In the desperate hope of being readmitted to communion, he began a passionate and detailed correspondence with Hafenreffer about his refusal in conscience to sign the Formula of Concord. After an exchange of two letters, Hafenreffer laid their correspondence before the theological faculty and the consistory for a decision. The time for discussion was over. On July 31, 1619, he delivered their official verdict: "Either you will abandon your erroneous and wholly fallacious fantasies and embrace the divine truth with humble faith, or stay away from the fellowship of our church and of our creed." Kepler was effectively excommunicated from the Lutheran church.

After his arrival in Linz in 1612, the first project upon which Kepler embarked was finding a new wife to care for his children and run his new household. He undertook this search in deadly earnest but with his characteristic inability to keep any one thing on his mind. Kepler's tortured route toward finding a bride is preserved in a letter to an unnamed noble friend, in which the various candidates are referred to only by number, which gives the procedure a comical mathematical overtone. He had called his many years of trial and error in planetary theory his "warfare with Mars." He likewise waged a battle in his mind over which candidate to pick.

Number One was a widow he and his wife had known in Prague, whom his wife had seemed to recommend before her death. It seemed fitting that a mature man like Kepler, now past the passion of youth, should settle down with a woman experienced in running a household. But she had two marriageable daughters and her assets were controlled by a trustee whom she did not want to alienate. Besides, though she looked healthy enough, her breath stank, and when Kepler saw her again after six years, he did not find her attractive. To confuse matters, one of her daughters had become Number Two in the interim, an unseemly turn of affairs. The daughter was attractive and well educated, but used to luxury and immature for running a household. She would be more glittering than useful. At this point, bewildered by the choice and questioning whether it was a good idea to consider what his wife would have wanted, Kepler had left Prague.

Putting those prospects aside, there was Number Three, another widow from Bohemia who was attractive and good with the children. She was willing, but betrothed to another, who had in the meantime gotten a prostitute pregnant, so she felt released from that obligation. But it did not work out.

The series continued in Linz with Number Four. She was from an honorable family, attractive and athletic in stature, and the match might well have gone through, had Kepler not been distracted by Five. Compared with Four, Five's family was less respectable and she had less property and a smaller dowry, but she distinguished herself with her seriousness and independence, and above all with her love and Kepler's faith in her humility, frugality, diligence, and love of the stepchildren.

Kepler vacillated, waiting for advice on whether he should marry Three after all. When he abandoned that prospect, he started to favor Four, but in the meantime she had grown tired of waiting and become engaged to someone else. By this time, Five was losing her luster as well. Number Six had a certain nobility, but she was immature and possibly conceited. He felt awkward abandoning Five and went back to her. But then friends, concerned with her common origins, recommended Number Seven, a noblewoman. She was a good candidate, but he could not make up his mind, so she rejected him.

By now the imperial mathematician's inept wooing had become the talk of Linz, but the parade of candidates went on. Number Eight had religious scruples due to Kepler's exclusion from communion. Number Nine had lung disease, and Kepler foolishly tested her by telling her he was in love with someone else. Number Ten was ugly and so fat that Kepler was afraid people would laugh at the comical contrast to his thinness. Finally, Number Eleven was with-drawn after a long wait because she was too young.

Five had long been in his mind. He summoned up his courage, returned to her, offered her his hand, and she accepted. She was Susanna Reuttinger, the orphaned daughter of a cabinetmaker, who had lived for many years as the ward of Baroness von Starhemberg, whose husband was one of Kepler's patrons in Linz. At 24 years old, she was much younger than Kepler's 41 years, which occasioned some twittering. Even Kepler's stepdaughter Regina wrote to say that Susanna was not old enough to act as stepmother to Kepler's children. But he loved and trusted her. They were married on October 30, 1613, and in time, she bore him seven more children, only one or two of whom survived to adulthood. We hear little more about her during his life, but in Kepler's life, no news is generally good news.

Though the document in which Kepler pours out to his noble friend the misadventure of selecting a new bride is pathetic, even comedic, Kepler found the process profound. He could do nothing more than question the role of divine providence in the series of events that tore him one way and then another before revealing his true love. Throughout, he had been diverted by considerations of his prospective bride's status, family encumbrances, wealth, and his standing in the community, but in the end he had chosen an honest common woman. His actions caused him to question his own character, as he asked, "Can I find God, Who in the contemplation of the entire universe I can almost feel in my hands, also in myself?"

Kepler eased back into scholarly work. Still unable to immerse himself in the astronomical work that consumed him, he addressed his skills to an interesting mathematical problem having to do with wine barrels. In the summer of 1613, Kepler was summoned to Regensburg by Emperor Matthias, who had succeeded Rudolf upon his death and confirmed Kepler's appointment as imperial mathematician

STEREOMETRIA DO-

fit, ut æquentur capacitate, quia vix vnquam profunditates ventrium ad diametrum orbis lignei, attingunt proportionem fefquitertiam. Hactenus de figura Dolij Auftriaci, fequitur,

De virga cubicâ eiufq; certitudine.

THEOREMA XXVI.

In dolijs, quæ funt inter fe figuræ fimilis: proportio capacitatum eft tripla ad proportionem illarum longitudinum, quæ funt ab orificio fummo, ad imum calcem alterutrius Orbis lignei.

Sint dolia diverfæ magnitudinis, fpecie eadem SQKT, XGCZ, quorum orificia OA, diametri orbium ligneorum QK, ST & GC, XZ, eo-

Schema XXII.

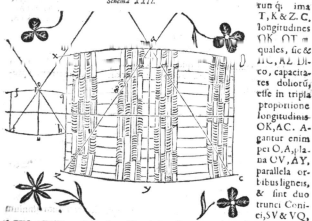

rumq; ima T, K & Z. C. longitudines OK, OT æquales, fic & AC, AZ Dico, capacitates doliorû, effe in tripla proportione longitudinis OK, AC. Agantur enim per O, A, plana OV, AY, parallela orbibus ligneis, & fint duo trunci Conici, SV & VQ,

fcXY, & YG inter fe fimiles. Quæ igitur de proportione dimidiorum doliorum funt vera, illa etiam de duplicatis erunt vera. Sint igitur propofitæ figuræ OVKQ. AYCG, conici trunci, fintq; latera figurarum OQ, VK, & AG, YC. Diametri Bafium minorum QK, GC, diametri bafium maiorum OV, AY; & OQKV, AGCY fectiones quadrilateræ figurarum per fuos axes, fimiles inter fe, earumq; diagonij OK, AC.

Ergò cum figuræ fimiles, fint ad feinvicem in tripla proportione analogorum laterum, erit proportionis AG lateris ad OQ latus, aut GC diametri, ad QK diametrum tripla, proportio GY corporis ad QV corpus. At in figuris planis trilateris AGC & QK fimilibus, ut GC ad analogum QK, vel ut AG ad analogum OQ, fic etiam diagonios AC ad analogon diago.

In Nova stereometria doliorum vinariorum *(1615), Kepler discussed the problem of the measurement of the volume of wine barrels. Wine merchants calculated the volume of a barrel from a linear measure of the diagonal from the fill hole (a) to the side of the bottom (z). Kepler simplified the process of measurement by treating the cask as the sum of two truncated cones.*

shortly thereafter. On the way back down the Danube to Linz, Kepler noticed that the banks of the river were lined with wine casks of various shapes and sizes and he became interested in the problem of how to express their volumes mathematically.

Since their sides were not straight, he had to think of a way to approximate their volume as the sum of a large number of thin disks, each of which was slightly larger or smaller than the next. In a characteristically Keplerian manner, he soon realized that similar techniques could be used to calculate the volume of whole families of solid figures. In particular, he wanted to generalize the study to include shapes generated by conic sections (the family of curves including the circle, ellipse, and parabola) rotated around any line in their plane. Though some of his demonstrations may have lacked mathematical rigor, this work became an important part of the history of the development of the integral calculus in the 17th century, even though it had the apparently prosaic title *Nova Stereometria doliorum vinariorum* (A New Stereometry of Wine Casks).

The book was not a tremendous success. In fact, after failing to interest any publisher, Kepler took the initiative of having a printer, Johannes Plank, brought to Linz and in 1615 the *Nova Stereometria doliorum vinariorum* became the first book ever published in the city. Kepler's superiors, the representatives of the Estates, were unimpressed, and they advised their mathematician to concentrate on the matters specified in the contract: the *Rudolfine Tables* and the map. Kepler had found working on the map uninteresting and odious, not least because, as he wrote in a report on his work, his information-gathering trips had been marred by "scolding and threats from inexperienced, coarse, and suspicious peasants." Besides, he argued, the map distracted his attention from the *Rudolfine Tables*. The representatives took the hint and transferred responsibility for the map to their district engineer.

His experience with the *Nova Stereometria doliorum vinariorum* had the important consequence of forcing Kepler to become his own publisher. In the following years, he fed Planck a series of works he composed in Linz. A German edition was prompted in part by having Planck sitting idle and also by the opportunity it presented of widening the circle of presentation copies for which Kepler would receive the customary financial reward. Such honoraria were often more lucrative than the actual sale of the book. In the case of the German edition, Kepler already had the woodblocks for the illustrations, so he only had to pay for new typesetting and printing. Once he had distributed the presentation copies and tallied up the honoraria he received in return, he covered the production costs and raked in at least 40 florins pure profit before actually selling a single copy. In addition, he resumed publishing annual prognostications in 1616 after a hiatus of 11 years. He considered this "a little more honorable than begging," and he needed the money for his next big publishing venture, an astronomical textbook.

Even during the composition of the *Astronomia nova,* it had been clear to Kepler that his new astronomy would be incomprehensible to most readers. In addition to being philosophically alien, the ellipse and the area law made calculations much more complicated. As early as 1611, Kepler had begun planning a more textbook-like exposition that would reach students down to "the low schoolbenches," and yet also contain the theoretical basis of the *Rudolfine Tables.*

He named the book the *Epitome astronomiae Copernicanae* (The Epitome of Copernican Astronomy) in conscious imitation of his own teacher Maestlin's oft-reprinted textbook, the *Epitome astronomiae.* But whereas Maestlin had taught introductory astronomy from a geocentric standpoint, Kepler became the first person to present heliocentric astronomy in textbook form. Kepler gave Planck the manuscript of the first volume in 1616, which contained basic material on the nature and scope of astronomy, the shape of the earth, the celestial sphere, the earth's motion around the sun, and the sun's consequent risings and settings, up to some problems in spherical trigonometry.

Immediately after finishing this volume, Kepler gave Planck his *Ephemeris for 1618.* An ephemeris ("ephemerides" is the plural) contains tables that give the position of each of the planets for every day of the year. Since ephemerides were essential reference books for astrologers and navigators, they were a lucrative product for astronomers of Kepler's time. The *Rudolfine Tables* would give the theory and means for anyone to calculate ephemerides that were just as accurate as his own, so Kepler got a head start on cashing in on their commercial potential by starting to calculate his own ephemerides before giving others the means to do so.

He had had a good theory for Mars in the *Astronomia nova*. When his life began to settle down in Linz in 1614, he had worked on the other planets off and on, and by May 1616, he was far enough along to begin grinding out ephemerides. But then, there was the problem of printing. Ephemerides were mostly numbers and printers did not normally have enough. Kepler therefore decided to invest in his own set of numerical type. The tedious calculations took time too. Kepler had help from assistants now and then but had to do much of it himself.

With the help of Kepler's type, Planck's press kept cranking. A prognostication for 1618 finished off 1617, to be ready for the new year. Then, in 1618, followed an ephemeris for 1617, an ephemeris for 1619, and a prognostication for 1619.

Even as Planck was clearing the backlog of publications, mounting troubles in Kepler's personal life diverted him from the task of completing the *Rudolfine Tables*. To begin with, the problem of his exclusion from communion weighed heavily on his mind. He began also to get wind of family problems back home in Württemberg. At the end of December 1615, he had gotten word from his relatives that accusations of witchcraft had been leveled against his 68-year-old mother. Almost a year later, to keep her from making matters worse for herself, they had sent her to Linz to live with her son.

The storm in Kepler's personal life mounted in the fall

of 1617. First, his two-and-a-half-year-old daughter Margarethe Regina, the first of his children with Susanna, died on September 8, 1617, of cough, consumption, and epilepsy. Shortly thereafter, her namesake, his stepdaughter Regina, died on October 4, 1617. She had been seven years old when Kepler married her mother, Barbara, and he had loved her from the start. Through the subsequent years in Prague as he battled with the theory of Mars, he had watched as she grew into a young woman. In 1608, he had seen her married in a good match to Philip Ehem, a descendant of a prominent Augsburg family, then representative at the imperial court of Elector Frederick IV of the Palatinate. In the disorder of 1610 they had moved back to the Palatinate, though she still kept in touch with her father in letters. She and her husband had just moved to Walderbach, near Regensburg, when she died at the age of twenty-seven.

Philip Ehem was desperate for help with Kepler's three grandchildren and begged him to send his eldest daughter, 15-year-old Susanna, to help him temporarily. Kepler agreed, and accompanied her personally on the trip up the Danube to Regensburg. From there, he went on to Württemberg, where his mother had gone earlier in the month, to see what he could do to put an end to the nonsense about sorcery.

As diversion on his trip, he took with him Vincenzo Galilei's *Dialogo della musica antica e moderne* (Dialogue Concerning Ancient and Modern Music), in which the astronomer Galileo's father had defended the Pythagorean theory of harmony. Kepler had long been interested in theories of harmony because of their mathematical basis. Though he found the Italian a little rough going, it was similar enough to Latin, and he read through three-quarters of it with relish during the trip.

The trip to Württemberg ended up being fruitless, as proceedings against his mother were once again delayed. He did get a chance to visit Tübingen, where he discussed every aspect of his new tables with old Maestlin and met an impressive young man, Wilhelm Schickard, who was not only mathematically talented but also an expert in oriental languages, such as Hebrew and Arabic. But Kepler's attempt to reconcile himself with Hafenreffer and his faith was rebuffed. On the way back, he stopped to visit Susanna to see how she was settling in, and then returned to Linz.

He arrived in Linz on December 22, 1617, just at the beginning of the Christmas festivities. The final blow came when he found his six-month-old daughter Katharina, his second child with Susanna, deathly ill, and on February 9, 1618, she, too, died. Kepler had lost three children in less than six months.

His spirit was too weighed down to go back to his work on the *Rudolfine Tables*, which he had broken off in the fall. Instead, he sought solace from the terrible dissonances in his personal life in another study, writing to a friend "Since the *Tables* require peace, I have abandoned them and turned my mind to developing the *Harmony*."

Kepler had first conceived of a work devoted to certain kinds of mathematical regularities in the world—which he called "harmonies"—during the dark period in 1599, after the death of his first daughter named Susanna and during the time when the measures against the Protestants in Styria were becoming ever more oppressive. He had sketched out his thoughts on mathematical harmony at that time in considerable detail, even going so far as to describe the structure of the book he would one day write.

When he succeeded in getting a copy of Claudius Ptolemy's *Harmony*—first in a Latin translation and then in a manuscript in the original Greek—he had been stunned by the similarity. That two men separated by a millennium and a half in time should converge on the same findings showed Kepler that he had surpassed time and space in his contemplation of the divine. "That the very nature of things was revealing itself to men through interpreters separated by the distance of centuries was the finger of God," he wrote.

The inquiry to which Kepler was returning in 1618 was the one he had turned to when his career changed from the church to science: to proclaim the glory of God from the Book of Nature. As in the *Mysterium*, he sought by revealing the underlying mathematical regularities in nature to make manifest the wisdom of its Creator. The unfamiliarity of the study should not make us think that Kepler resorted to mysticism, the irrational spiritual union with God. On the contrary, Kepler's work was supremely rational. Though his logic was strained at times by the effort to find the rational explanation underlying every aspect of harmony, he relentlessly pursued the questions until he had reasonable answers.

Harmony was the earliest human experience of fundamental mathematical relationships in nature. Already, in the 6th century B.C. the Pythagoreans had recognized the role of number in harmony with a religious awe. The first phenomena were those found in music. A string plucked once, then held down midway and plucked again, sounds an octave. The ratio of the length of the strings is 1:2. There are a limited number of additional harmonious tones. A ratio of 2:3 sounds a fifth, 3:4 a fourth, 3:5 a major third, 5:8 a minor third, 4:5 a major sixth, and 5:6 a minor sixth. But why these lengths, and why are they harmonious?

Harmony was also considered to be the explanation for the spacing of the distances of planets from the earth; the planets would be arranged at certain distances that corresponded to harmonic intervals. These harmonious spacings gave rise to the notion that there was a "music of the spheres."

The Pythagoreans and Plato saw the numbers as being fundamental. But Kepler never saw numbers, or quantities, as primary. Thus, when he asked why there were six and only six planets in the *Mysterium cosmographicum*, he did not ruminate on the significance of the number six. Instead, he saw geometry as primary. "Before the origin of things," he wrote, "geometry was coeternal with the divine Mind."

The foundation of his work on harmony therefore began with two substantial parts on geometry. He defined different levels of "knowability" for figures that could be constructed with the classical Euclidean tools of ruler and compass, the equilateral triangle, square, pentagon, hexagon, octagon, and a few others. Since the seven-sided heptagon was not constructable in this way, he reckoned God Himself could not have used it in the construction of the world. He expressed his conclusion best in a letter to a friend, where he wrote that, in the area of mathematics, "these things alone we know properly, and, if it can be said piously, with the same kind of comprehension as God, at least as much as we comprehend anything in this mortal life."

Much of the first two parts of Kepler's book was original mathematics. For instance, his definition of "congruence" was the foundation of a field of mathematics still actively practiced today. Kepler's "congruence" was the property of plane polygons to tessellate, or to fill a plane regularly and completely. Squares, triangles, and hexagons are perfectly congruent and can thus be used to tile floors, hence the modern name for this area of mathematics is "tiling theory." Kepler also published his discovery of two new perfect solids, the so-called star solids, both having 60 sides. But since they are constructed on top of Platonic solids (for instance by attaching a tetrahedron to each face of an icosahedron), Kepler considered them secondary in importance to the fundamental five Platonic solids.

Kepler applied his mathematics to musical harmony by arguing that only knowable polygons that divide the circumference of a circle into integral sections that are themselves the number of sides of knowable polygons form consonant proportions. For instance, the octagon and the pentagon are both knowable figures, that is, they are constructable with

ruler and compass. An octagon divides a circle into 8 equal arcs. Since the pentagon is also a knowable polygon, it is allowed to combine five of those arcs and to compare their length to the circumference of the circle. In this case, the ratio of lengths will be 5:8, the same as the ratio of strings in a minor third. On the other hand, since a heptagon is not a knowable polygon, the arcs combined in the ratio 7:8 will be inharmonious. The reason for both types of harmony came ultimately from the relation between God and His creation. As people are made in the image of God, so they have in them the inherent appreciation of consonant ratios determined by the knowable polyhedra, even if they are ignorant of mathematics.

The crowning part of Kepler's book on harmony was the fifth part, in which he addressed himself to the spacing of the planets and its relation to musical harmony. He had already argued in the *Mysterium cosmographicum* that God had based the spacing of the planets on the five Platonic solids. He did not now abandon that idea but sought to find the causes of two more phenomena. One was the size of the planetary eccentricities, that is, how far the sun is from the center of each of the planets' orbits. The eccentricity determines how close a planet gets to the sun at its closest approach, called "perhelion," and how far away it gets at its furthest distance, called "aphelion." Consequently, as governed by Kepler's second law, the eccentricity determines how quickly a planet moves at perihelion and how slowly it moves at aphelion. The eccentricities of the planets are not the same. Mars has a comparatively large eccentricity, while Venus has scarcely any eccentricity at all. Much as he had done some 20 years earlier in the *Mysterium cosmographicum*, Kepler set himself the problem of explaining why the planets had the seemingly arbitrary eccentricities they had. The second new phenomenon whose cause he sought had occupied his thoughts for 25 years. He wanted to know the precise mathematical relationship between the planets' mean distances from the sun and their orbital periods (how long it took for them to return to the same place in their orbits).

Kepler thought that the answer to both of these questions would be related to harmony. But a straightforward comparison of the various planets' closest (perihelial), mean, and furthest (aphelial) distances did not reveal harmonious relationships. Kepler now began another search for harmonious relationships between the planets' angular speeds as viewed from the sun. These could be within one planet's orbit, between its slowest speed at aphelion and its fastest speed at perihelion. If such a harmonious relationship existed, it would explain why the planet had the eccentricity it did. Or the relationship could exist between two planets, say between the aphelial speed of one and the perihelial speed of the next. Such a relationship would bear on the spacing of the planets with respect to one another. It was a vexing problem, but Kepler eventually succeeded in finding an arrangement that embodied all musical harmonies and corresponded to the planets' observed distances and eccentricities.

Kepler composed the book in a frenzy of activity during which every thought he had ever had about harmony came back to him and was included somewhere. At the very end, on May 15, 1618, the final piece of the puzzle fell into place. For 25 years, he had been seeking the relationship between the periods of the planets and their distances from the sun. It was as simple as imaginable: the ratio of the period squared over the distance cubed was the same for all planets. This was "Kepler's third law of planetary motion."

The fact that this final mystery was revealed to Kepler just as he was finishing up a book that was the culmination of his life's work made him exultant:

> Now, eighteen months since the twilight, three months since sunrise, but just a few days since the dazzling sunlight of my most wonderful contemplation shone forth, nothing can restrain me. I want to give in to the sacred frenzy, I want to taunt mortal men with my candid confession: I have stolen the golden vessels of the Egyptians to construct a tabernacle for my God far from the boundaries of Egypt. If you forgive me, I will rejoice. If you are incensed, I will endure. I am throwing the dice and writing the book, whether for my contemporaries or for posterity, it does not matter. It can await its reader for a hundred years, if God Himself waited six thousand years for His contemplator.

On May 27, 1618, Kepler put down his pen. His masterpiece, *Harmonices mundi libri V* (Five Books on the Harmony of the World) was complete. It was dedicated to King James I of England, whom Kepler had selected because he hoped that James might act as a peacemaker between Europe's warring faiths. He offered it so that his examples of the brilliant harmony God had put in His creation might give James strength in his quest for harmony and peace among the churches and the states.

However unrealistic that hope might have been, it was too late: four days earlier neighboring Bohemia had erupted into revolution, igniting the Thirty Years War.

The planets' periods had been known rather accurately for centuries. The relative distances of the planets were harder to determine, but Tycho Brahe's accurate observations had also provided Kepler with good values for the distances during his work on the *Rudolfine Tables*. These are the data Kepler had:

	Mercury	Venus	Earth	Mars	Jupiter	Saturn
Period	88	225	365	687	4,333	10,759
Distance	388	724	1,000	1,524	5,200	9,510

The periods are given in days, and the distances in $\frac{1}{1000}$ ths of the earth's average distance from the sun. If we convert the periods into years and define the earth's average distance to be 1 Astronomical Unit (A.U.), we have:

	Mercury	Venus	Earth	Mars	Jupiter	Saturn
Period	0.24	0.616	1.00	1.88	11.87	29.477
Distance	0.388	0.724	1.00	1.524	5.20	9.51

Already, we can see the relationship Copernicus noted, the clear correlation between the planet's distances and their periods. But Kepler was seeking an exact relationship between period and distance that would be the same for all of the planets. Let us begin by calculating the ratio of the period to the distance.

	Mercury	Venus	Earth	Mars	Jupiter	Saturn
$\frac{\text{Period}}{\text{Distance}}$	0.62	0.851	1.00	1.23	2.28	3.10

The spread in the values between Mercury and Saturn indicates that the ratio is not constant for all planets. Dividing another factor of distance into the denominator should increase Mercury's value while decreasing Saturn's value.

	Mercury	Venus	Earth	Mars	Jupiter	Saturn
$\frac{\text{Period}}{\text{Distance}^2}$	1.6	1.18	1.00	0.809	0.439	0.326

But now, we have gone too far the other way; the ratio for Saturn is smaller than that for Mercury. We will have to multiply another factor of period into the numerator.

	Mercury	Venus	Earth	Mars	Jupiter	Saturn
$\frac{\text{Period}^2}{\text{Distance}^2}$	0.38	0.724	1.00	1.52	5.21	9.61

At first, it might seem like we are not getting anywhere. The spread in the values is wider than when we started out. But the ratios look suspiciously similar to the planets' distances. Dividing one more factor of the distance into the denominator should even them out.

	Mercury	Venus	Earth	Mars	Jupiter	Saturn
$\dfrac{\text{Period}^2}{\text{Distance}^3}$	0.99	1.00	1.00	1.00	1.00	1.01

As though by magic, it works out that the period squared over the distance cubed is very nearly the same for all of the planets. This was the relationship linking the planets' individual periods and distances that Kepler had been seeking for 20 years.

Expressed in modern notation, Kepler's third law is that for all bodies orbiting another body,

$$\frac{p^2}{a^3} = k$$

where p is the period, a is the mean distance, and k is a constant that depends on the body being orbited and the units used. In the case above, for the solar system, using years and Astronomical Units, it just turns out to be $1.00 \; {}^{\text{year}^2}\!/_{\text{A.U.}^3}$. Other units will not yield such elegant constants. Nor is the constant the same for other orbital systems.

In 1618, irate Protestant representatives threw two Catholic regents and their secretary out of the window of the Hradschin in Prague. This act was the beginning of the Thirty Years War.

Witch Trial

On May 23, 1618, a gang of dissatisfied Protestant representatives had stormed the council chamber in the Hradschin in Prague, where they grabbed two Catholic officials and, in a time-honored Bohemian expression of revolt, threw them out of the castle window. This "defenestration of Prague," as it is called, marked the beginning of the Thirty Years War, an insane and devastating conflict that would lay waste to Germany as pillaging armies of ever-increasing size swept across her. In the process, one third of the population would be killed, either directly or indirectly from disease and starvation, and Germany would be reduced to a mere shadow of her former glory. By the time the warring parties had finally exhausted themselves and brought an end to the conflict with the Peace of Westphalia (1648), Kepler would be long dead.

Although the tensions came to a head in 1618, they had been building for some time. The conflict between the Catholics and the Protestants had put the delicate patchwork of duchies and principalities that made up the Holy Roman Empire under increasing strain. Even within the Hapsburg emperor's own hereditary lands, such as Upper and Lower Austria, there was considerable potential for religious conflict, with the powerful landed Estates being primarily Protestant while their sovereigns were Catholic. Archduke Ferdinand II had begun the process of converting his share of the family lands back to Catholicism, but they represented a small fraction. Outside the Hapsburg lands, the independent states of the empire formed self-defense pacts based on their faith, the Protestant Union (1608) and the Catholic League (1609). These pacts looked to coreligionists in countries outside the empire for monetary and military support, creating faultlines that would ensure that war, when it began, would involve all of Europe's major powers.

The war began with an uprising in Bohemia. The predominately Protestant Bohemians had long jealously defended their freedom of religion. In 1617, when they named Archduke Ferdinand II "king designate" to succeed Matthias upon his death, it was with the expectation that he would honor the concessions ensuring religious rights they had forced from his predecessors, Rudolf and Matthias. They had reason to regard Ferdinand with suspicion, since many of the refugees of his religious persecution had settled in Bohemia. The Bohemians soon came to regret their choice of Ferdinand as "king designate." When Ferdinand went to negotiate his claim to become the next emperor at the imperial court in Vienna—where Matthias had returned it, ending Prague's golden age as the capital of the empire—he left Prague in the hands of ten regents, seven of whom were Catholic, with explicit instructions to curb Protestant power.

In the spring of 1618, the Protestants summoned a meeting of the Bohemian Estates to discuss the anti-Protestant policies. The order came down from the Hradschin, where the Catholic regents sat, for the delegates to disperse. Such a command was regarded as unconstitutional. The delegates of the Estates responded by marching on the Hradschin and throwing two of the regents and their secretary out of the window. The revolt had begun.

While the Estates organized a provisional government and started to raise an army, Ferdinand organized a counter-attack, but it took time. In the meantime, Lusatia, Silesia, and Upper Austria joined the revolt in the summer of 1618. By the following summer, Moravia and Lower Austria had joined as well. In a stunning move, the rebel army marched south into Lower Austria and laid siege to the imperial capital Vienna. By then, Ferdinand had raised an imperial army of 30,000 men with help from the Spanish Hapsburgs and the Pope. They invaded southern Bohemia, cutting off the rebel army at Vienna and lifting the siege.

Political events now took center stage. In July 1619, the Estates of the Bohemian Crown signed a treaty of alliance with the Estates of Upper and Lower Austria. In the meantime, Matthias, emperor and king of the Bohemians, had passed away. In August, the Bohemians nullified Ferdinand's election as "king designate," and offered the crown to Frederick V, the prominent Calvinist prince of the Protestant Palatinate. At just the same time, a meeting of the seven imperial electors in Frankfurt elected Ferdinand II holy Roman emperor on August 28, 1619. Thereafter, he immediately went south to Munich for negotiations with Maximilian of Bavaria, the powerful leader of the Catholic League.

It was agreed that Maximilian's Catholic League forces would drive east into Bohemia through Upper Austria. At the same time, imperial troops from Vienna would attack the Bohemian forces in Lower Austria, and troops from the Spanish Netherlands would invade the Palatinate,

Holy Roman Emperor Ferdinand II fought with Protestants from his time as Archduke of Styria through his reign as emperor, creating a great deal of political unrest.

protecting the Bavarians' rear flank. On July 17, 1620, 30,000 Catholic League troops invaded Upper Austria. Recapturing Linz was their first objective.

For the Estates of Upper Austria, joining the Bohemian rebellion had been a foolhardy move. Once Linz was occupied by Bavarian forces, a swift retribution could be expected. Kepler immediately began worrying about his future. He had already experienced Ferdinand's Counter-Reformation measures once. On the other hand, though his appointment had not yet been confirmed by Ferdinand, he had been imperial mathematician to the two previous emperors for 18 years. This history and his ongoing work on the *Rudolfine Tables* tied him to the house of Hapsburg. But would he be able to continue his astronomical work and remain a Protestant?

In the fall of 1620, after Bavarian forces had taken the city, Kepler had to leave Linz to return to Württemberg. The course of his mother's witch trial demanded his presence. Because of the increasing uncertainty in Linz, he decided it was prudent to remove his family from harm's way, so he packed them up and took them with him as far as Regensburg, where he found them a place to stay. It was too shameful to tell anyone why he was going, so the Keplers left town secretly. Kepler did not even tell his assistant Gringalletus where they were going. When it was discovered that they were all missing, the people of Linz naturally assumed that the imperial mathematician and his family had fled the town for good.

The series of events that had now reached a climax in his mother's witch trial had begun more than five years before. It was a petty and sordid tale, one that had more to do with personal grudges, gossip, and intrigues involving money than sorcery. Even so, the supernatural connotation does not mean that it was an uncommon event. Indeed, the frequency of witch trials reached a frenetic peak in southern Germany in the late 16th and early 17th centuries. At the

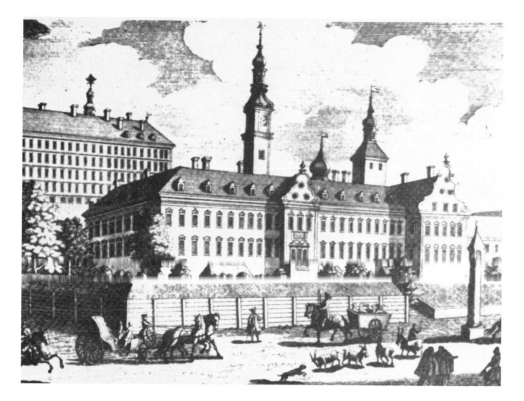

time when Kepler's mother's trouble began, no fewer than six women were sentenced to death in her town of Leonberg within a few months.

Frau Kepler's trouble was rooted in her unpleasant and meddling personality. Kepler himself conceded that she suffered from "trifling, nosiness, fury, and obstinate complaining," but he attributed such character flaws to the feeblemindedness of a seventy-year-old. Her avid interest in folk medicine and herbal cures also made her an easy target for accusations of witchcraft.

Her particular adversary was an unstable woman named Ursula Reinbold, the glazier's wife, whom Kepler called "the crazy." Frau Reinbold had had some unsatisfactory business dealings with Kepler's brother Christoph, the tinsmith. After a heated exchange, Christoph denounced her, upbraiding her with her record of imprisonment for prostitution. When Frau Reinbold complained to her friend Frau

The Landhaus, or country house, in Linz. The Protestant school where Kepler was hired to teach is behind and to the right; its tower is visible above the Landhaus.

Kepler about what her son had said, she got no support. Frau Kepler sided with her son, echoing his denunciation of her bad reputation. Frau Reinbold thereafter nursed a grudge against both of them.

Frau Reinbold made a habit of taking potions to abort illicit pregnancies. When one of these made her very ill, she attributed her sickness not to the drug, nor the botched treatment she had received from her brother, the court barber-surgeon of the prince of Württemberg, but to a "witch's drink" Frau Kepler had given her three and a half years earlier. Her brother, while drinking with the bailiff of Leonberg, Lutherus Einhorn, drunkenly insulted and threatened Frau Kepler. He went so far as to hold the tip of his sword to her throat, and threatened to run her through if she did not produce a "witch's antidote" for his sister. It was an impossible situation, for complying would have meant admitting that she was a witch. Standing her ground, though trembling all over, Frau Kepler energetically responded: she had not made Frau Reinbold sick, she said, and she could not make her better. Finally, Einhorn sobered up enough to put an end to the ugly scene.

Frau Kepler could not let this disgraceful encounter go unpunished. Unchallenged, the rumors of witchcraft Ursula Reinbold was spreading would fester and become ever more dangerous. In August 1615, with the support of her son Christoph and her son-in-law Georg Binder, a village pastor, she brought a libel suit against Ursula Reinbold for accusing her of being a witch. In October, Margarethe Binder, Kepler's sister, wrote to him in Linz informing him of these developments.

His sister's letter did not arrive until December 29. Kepler responded swiftly and decisively, writing an indignant letter to the Leonberg town senate on January 2, 1616. Mustering all of his status as imperial mathematician he strenuously objected to his mother's treatment, to the bailiff's behavior, and to the outrageous rumors that he, too, was somehow involved in "forbidden arts." He demanded that written copies of all legal proceedings involving his mother be forwarded to him.

Kepler had bitter suspicions that he himself was the origin of his mother's problem. A few years earlier, he had rewritten a student essay on heavenly appearances as viewed from the moon in the form of a playful piece of fiction. He had to give the narrator a way to find out about the moon, so he used the unfortunate literary device of having the narrator informed by a daemon summoned by the narrator's mother, an old woman skilled in folk magic. The similarity to Kepler's own mother was perhaps somewhat intentional but not to the point of implying that she was a witch. Kepler supposed that a handwritten copy of this little essay had found its way to Tübingen in 1611, where he imagined it had been "chattered about in barbers' shops." The court barber-surgeon would then have had good reason to suspect the imperial mathematician's mother of being a witch. In fact, however heartfelt Kepler's guilt, the essay may well have had little to do with the dark events in Leonberg.

In Leonberg, Lutherus Einhorn was in an awkward position. As bailiff he was the representative of the law in the town. But he had been a participant in the actions that precipitated Frau Kepler's suit. In order to avoid having to be a witness or reveal his part in them, he stalled the case of *Kepler* v. *Reinbold* as long as possible, so no evidence was scheduled to be taken before October 21, 1616.

Then, six days before the proceeding was scheduled to begin, matters took a turn for the worse. When Frau Kepler was out walking one day, she came across a group of girls carrying bricks to the kiln. The path was narrow, and the girls stepped aside to give a wide berth to the rumored witch. There was some kind of altercation. Frau Kepler claimed merely to have brushed their clothing and given them a dirty look. One of the girls claimed she had been hit on the arm, and that, thereafter, the pain increased hour by hour until she could not feel or move her hand.

Over the next two days, a conspiracy was hatched. The girl's mother, Walburga Haller, the wife of a day laborer, was in debt to Ursula Reinbold, and she and her family joined the Reinbold side. The barber-surgeon appeared on horseback from Tübingen. Suddenly, three days after the incident, Frau Haller went after Frau Kepler with a knife, screaming at her to heal her daughter. The Reinbolds and the Hallers wanted to press charges against her, so Frau Kepler was taken before the bailiff and interrogated. Einhorn examined the bruises on the girl's arm. After a convenient consultation with his friend the barber-surgeon, he authoritatively concluded, "It is a witch's grip; it's even got the right impression."

Frau Kepler now did a very foolish thing. She approached the bailiff with the offer of a silver goblet if he would forget about the whole incident and get on with taking evidence in her lawsuit. It was just what the bailiff needed to avoid exposing his part in the earlier attack on Frau Kepler. He suspended her case, and forwarded the charges of "witch's drink," "witch's grip," and bribery to the High Council in Stuttgart. The councilors returned the order to arrest her on sight, interrogate her, and "examine her strenuously" with regard to the accusations against her and her theological beliefs. It was the preliminary stage of a witch trial.

By the time the arrest order came back from Stuttgart, Frau Kepler had been hustled off to safety, first to her daughter's house in Heumaden and from there to Linz, where she stayed with her son from the end of 1616 to September 1617. When he heard about the turn of affairs, Kepler took the case into his hands. He immediately hired lawyers for his mother in Leonberg and for himself in Tübingen and Stuttgart. And he wrote a letter to the duke of Württemberg's vice chancellor detailing the bailiff's bias and bad behavior in the case and denying the rumors that his mother had fled jurisdiction because of her bad conscience.

In the fall of 1617, Kepler accompanied his mother home and attempted to get her civil suit in motion, but to no avail. The proceeding was delayed by the Reinbolds' legal maneuvering, possibly assisted by the barber-surgeon's influence at the ducal court in Stuttgart. At least, the interest in arresting and interrogating Frau Kepler seemed to have passed. Kepler finally had to suspend his effort and returned to Linz in early 1618. Things were moving very slowly.

The following summer, Kepler received a letter from his old classmate Christoph Besold, now a member of the law faculty at Tübingen and probably his lawyer there. Besold mentioned a danger to watch out for: the Reinbolds and the bailiff might contrive things so that Frau Kepler's civil suit could be turned around and become a criminal charge of witchcraft against her. He turned out to be exactly right. In October 1619, the Reinbolds filed a counter civil suit against Frau Kepler, demanding 1,000 florins in damages for poisoning Frau Reinbold with the "witch's drink." In effect, they were defending themselves against the libel charge by demonstrating that she really *was* a witch.

Their 49-count indictment against her was made possible by the flood of gossip unleashed by rumors of Frau Kepler's witchcraft. Everyone, it seemed, remembered some eerie, unnatural encounter with Frau Kepler. Among other things, she was supposed to be responsible for the death of pets and livestock, to have ridden a calf to death, to have attempted to lure a young girl to witchcraft, to have caused mysterious pains without touching people, to have passed through locked doors, to have killed infants by saying a blessing over their cribs, and to have asked the gravedigger for her father's skull so she could have it set in silver to be a goblet for her son, the mathematician. The last of the charges had the distinction of at least being true. Her defense was that she had heard of the ancient custom of making cups from deceased relatives' skulls in a sermon.

The legal situation had become very dangerous. With the bailiff on their side, testimony in the case of *Reinbold* v. *Kepler* began almost immediately, in November 1619. Thirty or forty witnesses were called, and their testimony was taken down in thick volumes.

In July 1620, the Reinbolds succeeded in getting the duke to turn their complaint into a criminal case. The high council ordered that Katharina Kepler be arrested and interrogated, under torture if necessary. In order to avoid commotion, on August 7, 1620, she was roused from her sleep, bundled into a large chest, and carried out of Heumaden in the dead of night.

The sudden turn of events disheartened the Kepler camp. Christoph Kepler and Georg Binder, Margarethe's husband, were ready to abandon Frau Kepler to her fate. They had too much to lose. Christoph was a young man and could not endure the shame of the community. It was more than he could take to have the spectacle of his mother's witch trial under his nose in Leonberg. He succeeded in having the trial transferred to Güglingen. Georg Binder was a pastor and had his position in the church to think about.

Margarethe seems to have been the only one who still held out hope. She wrote at once to her brother Johannes, telling him that his mother needed his help. He, in turn, wrote from Linz to the duke of Württemberg, asking him to stay the trial until he could arrive. It was his "God-given and natural right," he wrote, to come to his mother's aid. The trial was delayed five to six weeks. On September 26, 1620, Kepler met with his mother in prison.

The poor, bewildered, now-74-year-old woman was kept in chains, watched over by two hired guards, whom she had to pay out of her own pocket. She likewise had to pay her upkeep during the delay of the trial. These expenses revealed the naked greed of the Reinbold camp. Part of the reason for their suit had always been the hope of cashing in on Frau Kepler's assets. They had petitioned early on to have her property inventoried. When it now turned out that the two lackeys being paid to watch her were wastefully using firewood, threatening with their expenses to consume all of her assets during the trial, Frau Reinbold petitioned "in the name of God's mercy" to protect the defendant's funds.

Kepler took charge of the defense. There is a funny note in the transcripts of the trial that attests to the force of his presence. "The prisoner," the scribe writes, "appears *unfortunately* with the support of her son Johannes Kepler, the mathematician." Kepler directed his mother's lawyer, Johannes Rueff, to do all of his arguments in written form. It was a slower and costlier way of proceeding, but he had been advised that it more often led to a positive outcome. It can hardly be believed, therefore, that he was criticized by his brother Christoph for the higher costs. Kepler and Rueff submitted their written defense on October 2. The bailiff of Güglingen, sensing that he was being outmaneuvered, brought in Hieronymous Gabelkofer, the prince's counsel, to prosecute for the state.

New witnesses were heard in January 1621. In May, the defense submitted further written arguments. At this point, Kepler went to the capital, Stuttgart, to work on the final summation with his lawyer. Their conclusion was a 126-page brief rebutting all of the charges. Although composed with legal assistance, elements of it are in Kepler's hand and much of it represents his own work. It was very much his presence and his effort writing in his mother's defense that began to turn the balance.

The concluding defense was submitted on August 22. As was usual, the trial proceedings were sent to the law faculty at the University of Tübingen for a decision. Luckily, Kepler's ally, Christoph Besold, would be able to exert some inside influence there. It is perhaps an indication of the difficulty of escaping charges of witchcraft that, even after Kepler's devoted efforts and with Besold on the inside, they were still not able to achieve an acquittal. The best the court could decide was that it was not certain. It ordered that Frau Kepler be examined again under the lightest form of torture, the "territio verbalis," verbal terrification.

On September 28, 1621, the verdict was carried out as ordered. Against her protestations, Frau Kepler was taken to the appointed place in the company of Bailiff Aulber, three representatives of the court, and a scribe and was presented to the torturer. He showed her his instruments and, under threat of great pain and suffering, strenuously commanded her to tell the truth. She denied any involvement with witchcraft. The report of the bailiff reads, "She announced one should do with her what one would. Should one pull one vein after another out of her body, she knew that she had nothing to say. With that, she fell on her knees, said the Lord's prayer, and declared that God should make a sign if she were a witch or a demon or ever had anything to do with sorcery. Should she be killed, God would see that the truth came to light and reveal after her death that injustice and violence had been done to her, for she knew that He would not take His Holy Spirit from her but would stand by her."

In light of her testimony under threat of torture, the charges were dismissed. On October 3, 1621, the duke of Württemberg ordered that she should be set free. Of the outstanding costs of the trial, Jacob Reinbold was ordered to pay 10 florins for having initiated the proceedings and Christoph Kepler was to pay 30 florins for having incurred extraordinary expenses by having them transferred to Güglingen. Her spirit broken by the ordeal, Katharina Kepler died six months later, on April 13, 1622.

Immediately after his mother's interrogation, Kepler returned to Linz. The Linz Kepler returned to in November 1621 was far different from the one he had left. Shortly after his departure, Frederick V and the Bohemian

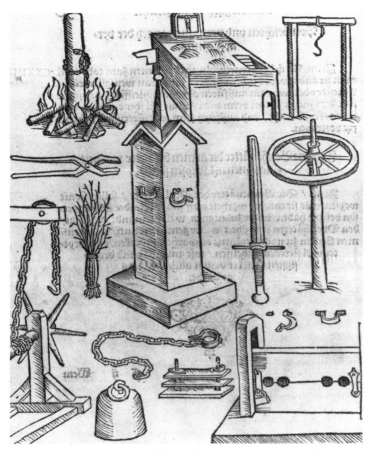

The standard tools of the torturer, as shown in this 16th-century wood-cut, included the strap-pado (bottom left), thumbscrews (bottom center), the Catherine wheel (bottom right), and the stake (top left). Kepler's mother was shown the tools and instructed in their use during her final inter-rogation.

rebel army had been swiftly defeated at the Battle of White Mountain. The Protestant revolution in Bohemia and the Austrian territories along the Danube had been repressed.

The city was still under occupation by the Bavarian army, and Ferdinand II would make use of their presence to stage a replay of the Counter-Reformation moves he had made in Styria 20 years before. For the time being, it was the prominent Protestant leaders of the rebellion he was after. In June, 27 Protestant ringleaders had been executed in Prague. Kepler's old friend Jessenius had been among them; he had had his tongue cut out before being quar-tered. A dozen of their heads were put on pikes on the bridge tower, where they remained as mute warnings for ten years before they disintegrated and fell off. In Linz, the actions were less lethal. Among other people, Kepler's nemesis Daniel Hitzler was thrown in prison.

Kepler found himself in a strange position. It had been widely known that his brother Protestants in Linz had rejected him. Now, when they were being oppressed, he was being spared. Still, his open admiration of Frederick V's father-in-law, James I, in the dedication of the *Harmonice mundi* and his sudden flight the previous year had given rise to rumors that the emperor had put a price on his head. His equally sudden reappearance was a real surprise. It was surprising to Kepler that almost the first thing that happened upon his return was that Ferdinand II confirmed his appointment as imperial mathematician on December 30, 1621.

As imperial mathematician, Kepler was left unmolested even while measures were taken the next year against other Protestant teachers and preachers. And then, a few years later, when all the rest of the Protestants were required to convert or leave (as they had been many years before in Styria), not only was Kepler allowed to stay but his printer Planck as well and as many skilled assistants as Planck needed.

By 1622, Kepler's many years of work on the *Rudolfine Tables* were beginning to come to an end. To many astronomers, it was about time. To them, it seemed that work on books like the *Harmonice mundi* or the second edition of the *Mysterium cosmographicum* (1621) had been a distraction from Kepler's "important" work of composing new astronomical tables based on Tycho Brahe's observations. To them, Kepler replied, "Do not sentence me completely to the treadmill of mathematical calculations, and leave me time for philosophical speculations, which are my only delight." But by the end of 1623, Kepler felt as though he were going through labor pains, "The *Rudolfine Tables*, which I received from Tycho Brahe as the father, I have now carried and formed within me for 22 whole years, as little by little the foetus forms in the mother's body. Now the labor pains torment me."

Hie sicht man die 12. Köpff auff den Prager Bruckenthurn auffgesteckt.

Part of the torment was finding a suitable place to print them. To Ferdinand, it was an important sign of normalcy that the astronomical achievement that had been supported by the Hapsburg house for so long should be printed in Austria. He would not allow Kepler to have the book printed in Ulm, where it was peaceful and there were more experienced printers. Money was also a problem, which led Kepler on a ten-month wild-goose chase from the imperial treasury in Vienna to various cities that were supposed to turn imperial payments over to Kepler but would not. He finally returned to Linz in the fall of 1625 with little to show for his travels. He was left with no alternative but to try out Planck and see how he would handle the high-prestige job of printing the imperial *Rudolfine Tables*. But before they could even get started, Linz erupted in civil disorder.

On October 10, 1625, Ferdinand II's government decided to become serious about the measures they were taking against the Protestants. The familiar pattern of repression from Styria was repeated in Linz. The previous expulsion of teachers and preachers had had time to take effect. It was now renewed with the threat of capital punishment. It was time to force the people to convert, too. All avenues for Protestant practice were forbidden. The measures culminated in the order that all people convert to Catholicism or leave the land by Easter 1626. Because of his position, Kepler was exempted from all of these measures. His only annoyance was that the Catholic Reformation Commission sealed his personal library on the grounds that it might contain heretical books. Ironically, when Kepler's friend the Jesuit Paul Guldin wanted to borrow a book, he had to tell him he could not get into his own library.

In the spring of 1626, Upper Austria reached a breaking point. Five thousand Bavarian troops still occupied Linz as surety for the debt owed Maximilian by Ferdinand II for his part in repressing the Bohemian rebellion. In lieu of interest on the debt, the Bavarians taxed Upper Austria. For his part, Ferdinand was relying on their presence to keep a lid on the country while he carried out his plan for compulsory conversion to Catholicism. This put the Bavarian occupiers in a dangerously unstable position. On May 15, 1626, in retaliation for the harrassment of Italian priests who had been brought in to return the parishes of Upper Austria to Catholicism, the leader of the Bavarian authorities ordered the summary execution of 17 randomly selected men. A peasant uprising erupted, which all but succeeded in driving the Bavarians and Ferdinand's forces out of Upper Austria.

The peasants formed themselves into large troops and roamed Upper Austria, burning and looting. On June 24, 1626, they besieged the capital, Linz. "By the help of God and the protection of His angels, I survived the siege intact," Kepler wrote to a friend. But the two months spent behind city walls waiting for the arrival of imperial relief forces had been an ordeal. Kepler's house was part of the city wall, and it was constantly occupied by soldiers who disturbed him with their comings and goings at all times of the day and night.

Worse still, shortly after the beginning of the siege, on June 30, the peasants started a fire in the outskirts of the city. Luckily, as the fire spread, no harm came to the hand-written copy of the *Rudolfine Tables* on which Kepler had worked so long. But the fire did consume Planck's press. With the press gone, there was no longer any reason to remain in Linz. Linz had gone from the peaceful haven Kepler had come to 11 years before to a repressive and disturbed place. When the siege was lifted in August, he wrote to the emperor requesting permission to leave. By November 20, he and his family were on a boat traveling up the Danube, and Kepler was looking for another place to print the *Rudolfine Tables*.

The frontispiece from Kepler's Rudolfine Tables (1627) shows the contributions of various astronomers. In the center, Tycho Brahe (with arm raised) and Copernicus (seated) discuss the merits of the Tychonic system. Kepler is shown in the lower left panel.

The Dream

When the storm is raging and the shipwreck of the state is threatening, there is nothing nobler for us to do than let down our anchor of peaceful studies into the depths of eternity.

—from a letter to Jacob Bartsch, November 6, 1628

With the onset of winter, November was not a very advantageous month for moving, but Kepler was possessed by the desire to be away from the disorder in Linz and to get on with the publication of the *Rudolfine Tables*. The boat carrying the Kepler family got as far up the Danube as Regensburg, but beyond there the river was iced over. Regensburg had by now become a familiar refuge for them, so Kepler settled his family there, loaded his type onto a wagon, and set out alone for Ulm.

When he got there on December 10, 1626, Kepler moved in across the street from Jonas Saur's printing shop. Having constant access to the shop was a necessity. Kepler had completed the 538-page manuscript, but it was complicated enough—especially with the layout of the many tables—that the author himself was needed on hand at all times. All the materials were in readiness as well. During his fruitless travels the previous year trying to collect his back salary, Kepler had ordered four bales of paper from the cities of Memmingen and Kempten in the expectation that he could barter for them with written orders from the emperor for the cities to pay him. But as it turned out, he ended up paying for the paper out of his own pocket. Anticipating that he would be allowed to print the *Rudolfine Tables* in Ulm, he had had it delivered directly there. He himself had brought along his set of numerical type and the special astro-nomical-symbol type he had had custom-molded for the *Rudolfine Tables*.

Despite some friction over cost, the printing proceeded at a frantic pace. Kepler had set the goal of completing the printing in time for the fall 1627 book fair in Frankfurt. He supervised the layout of the tables and proofread the sheets as they came out of the press. There were to be no errors. He wanted the tables to be perfect, a fitting capstone of his collaboration with Tycho Brahe and of his career as an astronomer.

There were still some details to be worked out. The book would need a dedication to the emperor from Brahe's heirs, who still had not been paid in full for Tycho's observ-ing logs and so still owned them. Kepler wrote informing them that the book was being printed. Tycho had begun the work and it was based on his lifetime of observations, so he would be listed on the title page as the primary author, where he was called "that Phoenix of astronomers." Even though it was Kepler who had written the entire book, he did not begrudge Tycho this honor in any way.

In addition, the *Rudolfine Tables* would be Kepler's first book with a frontispiece, a common feature of 16th- and 17th-century books. A frontispiece was a magnificent engraving that was packed with symbolism and meaning. Kepler had Schickard draw up a sketch of what he wanted and sent it to Tycho's heirs for approval.

The frontispiece as it finally appeared was a representation of a temple to Urania, the muse of astronomy. The development of astronomy is represented by the 12 columns supporting the roof. In the rear, where the columns are only rough-hewn logs, stands a Babylonian astronomer making an observation using only his fingers. He represents the ancient Babylonian observations to which astronomy traced its roots. Nearer the front, where Hipparchus and Ptolemy are seated, the columns are brick, representing the improvement in astronomy in ancient Greece. Copernicus has an Ionic column. And Tycho Brahe has a magnificent Corinthian column, on which his sophisticated instruments are hanging. In the center, Copernicus and Tycho discuss the merits of the heliocentric and Tychonic systems, with Tycho pointing toward the ceiling of the temple where his system is depicted and asking "Quid si sic?" or "What if it is like this?"

Standing around the roof of the temple are allegorical figures who assisted Kepler with his accomplishment. To the right are Magnetica with her compass needle and Stathmica with her balance and lever. They represent the celestial physics upon which Kepler's reform of astronomical theory was based. Then there are Kepler's mathematical helpers, Geometria and Logarithmica, who has the natural log of one half in her halo. On the left are the optical parts of astronomy, one of them holding the recently-invented telescope. Above them flies an eagle wearing the imperial crown dropping coins from its beak. It represents the three Hapsburg emperors who provided financial support for the project.

There was one aspect of the frontispiece that was not in the sketch shown to the heirs, with whom Kepler had always had difficulty. Below the figures in the base of the temple are panels depicting different scenes. In the center, for instance, is a map of Tycho's island Hven, where his observatory was located. And to the left is Kepler himself. He is looking out at the viewer, seated at a table under a banner listing his publications *Mysterium cosmographicum*,

Astronomiae pars optica, *Commentarium Martis* (that is, the *Astronomia nova*), and *Epitome astronomiae Copernicanae*. He is working by candlelight, having sketched some numbers on the tablecloth. On the table is his project: a model of the roof of the temple itself. Kepler has made a subtle but unmistakable statement about his role in this undertaking: though those on whom he based his work occupy places of honor on the stage above him, it is Kepler alone who is the architect of this achievement.

And it was a magnificent achievement. The tables them-

This detail of the frontispiece of the Rudolfine Tables *shows Kepler as the architect of the achievement. He works by candlelight on a model of the temple above him. The banner lists his important publications. A few coins dropped by the Hapsburg eagle have reached his desk.*

selves provided the means to calculate the position of any planet for any time thousands of years into the future or the past. It was only the third truly new set of planetary tables in European history. And whereas Copernicus's and Ptolemy's tables were more or less equally accurate, Kepler's were some 50 times more so. Within a few years, it was possible to pinpoint the time of a transit of Mercury across the face of the sun so that it was possible to observe it in transit for the first time in human history. It would be a spectacular demonstration of the accuracy of Kepler's tables. Of course, Kepler's theories were more difficult, especially since he had incorporated logarithms, which had only been invented a few years earlier. Much of the book, therefore, was made up of explanatory text that told the reader how to use the tables. There were also a geographical register of the longitudes and latitudes of the earth's major cities and Tycho Brahe's catalogue of the positions of 1,000 stars.

The printing of the *Rudolfine Tables* was finished on time in September 1627, and on September 15, Kepler set out with the copies for the Frankfurt fall book fair. He left the copies with the publisher Gottfried Tampach to sell on commission at an agreed-upon price, but he was not optimistic that sales would be brisk, noting, "There will be few purchasers, as is always the case with mathematical works, especially in the present chaos."

By the end of November, he was reunited with his family in Regensburg. Nearly a year had passed since he had left them to print the *Tables*. For many months, he had been thinking about what to do after the *Tables* were finished. During the summer, a series of imperial decrees had been issued, ordering the discharge of all non-Catholic officials in Upper Austria. Kepler had often escaped this sort of decree, but with the tables now finished, there was reason to think that the emperor might really fire him.

It was with some trepidation that Kepler went to the imperial court just after Christmas to present a copy of the

Duke Albrecht Wallenstein is received at the imperial court after defeating King Christian IV of Denmark. Wallenstein was immensely successful but a threat because of his power.

Rudolfine Tables to the emperor personally. He found the court in high spirits. By virtue of Ferdinand's ceaseless and creative diplomacy and major victories on the battlefield, the Protestant revolt had been completely put down. To seal their victory, Ferdinand had brought the court to Prague, where he was overseeing the installation of his son as king of Bohemia.

Much of the credit was due to the emperor's new favorite, General Albrecht Wallenstein. Born and educated as a Lutheran, Wallenstein set a course for success when he converted to Catholicism in 1606, which enabled him subsequently to marry an elderly widow with vast land holdings in Moravia. Wallenstein used his new-found wealth to good advantage, supporting Ferdinand II in putting down the Bohemian rebellion in 1619–1621. His financial speculation in the aftermath of the rebellion gave him the money to buy up 60 estates of banished or executed Protestant noblemen. Soon, he owned almost all of the northwestern quarter of Bohemia. His immense resources enabled him to speculate financially in warfare. With Ferdinand's blessing, he raised an imperial army of 24,000 men without charge to the treasury; the army would pay for itself with booty and tribute from conquered territories. Following the trend of the Thirty Years' War, his army soon numbered more than 100,000 men. Ferdinand, who was then no longer militarily dependent on Maximilian of Bavaria, gave Wallenstein the title of supreme commander of imperial troops and shortly thereafter elevated him to be Duke of Friedland.

Wallenstein was immensely successful as a general. In association with the commander of Catholic League forces, Count von Tilly, Catholic forces were able to defeat various Protestant threats through the mid- to late-1620s, most importantly invasions from the north by the Protestant King Christian IV of Denmark. In late 1627, when Kepler arrived at the imperial court, they were just celebrating Wallenstein's total victory over the Danish king. Christian had not only been driven off German soil but entirely off the Danish peninsula of Jutland. As his reward, Wallenstein was immediately given the Silesian principality of Sagan and was subsequently also made Duke of Mecklenburg.

Kepler's experience of the unhappy state of affairs in Linz had deceived him about what to expect at the imperial court. He was surprised to find that he had many admirers and well-wishers at the court in Prague. Some of them, of course, were old friends and acquaintances from his previous years there, although there was a sobering absence of any Protestants. The court had been as decisively cleansed as the lands under Ferdinand's control.

The emperor received Kepler graciously, pronouncing himself well pleased with the tables. The notion that Kepler might already have lost his job in the wake of the previous summer's imperial decrees was laughed off. In fact, for his 25 years of effort on the *Rudolfine Tables*, Kepler was given a grant of 4,000 florins, worth ten years' salary. Of course, Kepler had learned that a grant from the emperor was an unreliable asset. As it was, it brought the amount of money the emperor owed him to nearly 12,000 florins. If he ever hoped to collect on that debt, how could he leave imperial service?

However, Ferdinand did make it clear that the condition of his future service in the Hapsburg's lands was firmly conditional on Kepler's conversion to Catholicism, and the Jesuit Paul Guldin was assigned the task of convincing Kepler to convert. Needless to say, Guldin was unsuccessful. But there was another possibility. Kepler could remain in imperial service in one of the lands now held by General Wallenstein. Wallenstein himself had declared that he believed in the peaceful coexistence of the different faiths, a point of view with which Kepler agreed heartily. And the open practice of Protestant religion was still allowed in Wallenstein's Silesian duchy of Sagan.

Kepler and Wallenstein had a relationship of sorts going back 20 years. In 1608, Kepler had cast a horoscope for an anonymous nobleman. On the basis of the birth information, he described the man as "alert, quick, industrious," uninterested in ordinary things, brutal, hard on his subjects, and so forth. But also, he wrote, "with him can also be seen great thirst for glory and striving for temporal honors and power, by which he would make many great, dangerous, public and concealed enemies for himself but also he would mostly overcome and conquer these." It was a good description of Wallenstein, who had secretly commissioned it. Sixteen years later, after the Thirty Years War had begun, and Wallenstein had begun to amass those "temporal honors and power," Kepler received his first horoscope back, with the request for certain elaborations. He updated the horoscope but stopped with the year 1634 due to some "horrible disorder" in that year. In an eerie coincidence, 1634 would turn out to be the year in which Wallenstein was murdered.

The advantage of having Kepler working for him was that the ambitious general would have state-of-the-art astrological advice. Kepler himself had long recognized the inherent danger in providing astrological advice to men of great military and political power and had strenuously resisted being put in that position, so he and Wallenstein probably worked out an arrangement in which Kepler would supply the planetary positions—for which he was now the undisputed master—and the interpretation would be done by somebody else, probably Wallenstein's personal astrologer

Kepler prepared this horoscope for Wallenstein in 1608. Surrounding the center box are 12 triangles representing the astrological houses. House I (left) is ascendant, the most important house, containing the stars about to rise at the time of birth. It contains Saturn and Jupiter, which would be considered the important planets governing Wallenstein's character.

Gianbattista Zeno.

Kepler would also be a status symbol for Wallenstein, whose growing collection of duchies were rewards for his military victories. Wallenstein's support of Kepler's studies would show that he was not only a military strongman but also a civilized patron of the arts and sciences. Indeed, Wallenstein later tried to move Kepler to his newly-acquired city of Rostock, so that Kepler's presence might raise the status of the university there.

The outlines of an agreement were struck in February 1628 but were not finalized until April. Kepler would receive a house in Sagan, a printing press, and a rich stipend of 1000 florins a year. His duties were not spelled out but were minimal. In addition, Ferdinand "requested" that Wallenstein take into his own hands the problem of collecting the 11,817 florins Kepler was owed by the imperial treasury. In the past, Kepler had been written drafts on imperial cities that the cities had not honored. They were little better than bounced checks. The warrior Wallenstein might have more success. With the job and Wallenstein's responsibility for the collection of Kepler's back pay, as of the summer of 1628, it was clear that Kepler's future lay in Wallenstein's hands.

In May, Kepler returned to his family in Regensburg. The following month, he sent them on to Prague with their possessions while he himself traveled for one last time to Linz. Again, he was well received. He was even paid 200 florins for his presentation copy of the *Rudolfine Tables*, a generous gesture Kepler had not expected from a country so stricken by the recent war. Kepler described what had happened since leaving the city, including his arrangements with Wallenstein, and requested to be released from his contract. His request was granted, and afterwards he traveled immediately north to Prague to meet his family. Together, they traveled north to Sagan, where they arrived on July 20.

Kepler never felt at home there. He could barely understand the dialect of the local people, and his own German was regarded as barbarous. Sagan also had no intellectual culture to speak of, so he was almost completely unknown and he felt like a fish out of water. The combined effect was to make him feel very lonely. Idleness added to his discontent when the promised printing press was so slow to appear that even a year after his arrival it had not been provided. In the meantime, he made arrangements to use a press in nearby Görlitz, but he had to set all the type himself by hand. Only around the beginning of 1630 was he able to put a typesetter and a printer to work at his own personal press.

In an almost unimaginably heart-wrenching turn of events, Kepler's arrival in Sagan coincided with the beginning of the Counter-Reformation there. Though Sagan was almost exclusively Protestant and Wallenstein personally believed in the coexistence of the faiths, the political reality of working for Ferdinand II demanded that he comply. Needless to say, forced conversions on this massive scale were accompanied by bitter resentment and suffering. To Kepler, the measures unfolded in a predictable sequence, as the Protestant school gave way to one founded by Jesuits specially brought in for the purpose, "heretical" books were seized, Protestants were forbidden the practice of their religion, and finally those who refused to convert were ordered to leave. Kepler was again exempted, but experiencing the calamity of the Counter-Reformation for a third time could not have been easy.

To ease his loneliness and isolation, Kepler relied on his correspondence, especially with his good friend Matthias Bernegger in Strasbourg and with Wilhelm Schickard in Tübingen. This link to the outside world became all the more important when Bernegger began to play an active role in the wedding plans of Kepler's daughter Susanna. The prospective bridegroom was a young scholar of mathematics and medicine named Jacob Bartsch, who had gained Kepler's respect by publishing an ephemeris based on the inquiries into the kind of life he had led, how much money he spent, etc. Much of the planning for the match went on in a three-way correspondence between Kepler, Bernegger, and Bartsch. Indeed, Bartsch was well on the way to getting engaged to Susanna before even meeting her. But Kepler did require that in addition to his blessing, Susanna would have to approve of the match.

When it came time to plan the wedding itself, Kepler decided that the best place to hold it would be in Strasbourg. It was too far for him to travel, so Bernegger stood in for him, acting as the father of the bride. Kepler could only read the glowing account of the festivities that Bernegger wrote to him. The wedding was celebrated on the afternoon of March 12, 1630, after Bartsch had received his medical degree that very morning. Kepler's brother Christoph, his sister Margarethe, and his son Ludwig had all been there. The astronomer's daughter in the midst of her bridesmaids "shone out like the moon among the smaller stars," Bernegger reported. Huge crowds lined the street and Strasbourg's elite made up the wedding procession. "It was meant," Bernegger had to remind him, "especially to honor you."

Jacob Bartsch married Kepler's daughter Susanna in 1630. Bartsch was the first person to publish ephemerides based on the Rudolfine Tables.

In addition to the distance and his age—he was then 59—one other thing had kept Kepler from the wedding festivities in Strasbourg: his wife Susanna was eight months pregnant. The following month on April 18, she gave birth to a baby girl, Anna Maria, her seventh child, counting the two who had died in infancy. She now had two grown stepchildren and five of her own.

At the beginning of April, Kepler had spent some weeks consulting with Wallenstein. Tending to his wife after she gave birth also took Kepler away from the print shop, and without his presence, the printing of his next batch of ephemerides could not proceed. Kepler therefore instructed them to get to work on his book about the moon, entitled *Somnium* (The Dream).

The *Somnium* was a project that Kepler had begun more than 25 years earlier, when he was a student at Tübingen. As we have seen, when he was a student, he was convinced that Copernicus's heliocentrism was true. But he ran into trouble convincing people of its truth because they could not imagine that the earth was moving without feeling it. In order to highlight the ambiguous experience of the observer, in 1593 he composed an essay on what the celestial appearances would look like for beings on the moon.

He had kept the essay, and some years later in Prague, he expanded it into a piece of fiction, full of double meanings and clever allusions that would delight his learned friends in the imperial court. This was the essay he thought was responsible in part for his mother's witch trial. Once she was freed, he decided that he would avenge the gossip about his story by publishing it openly with explanatory notes that would show everyone just how foolishly it had been taken out of context and inflated. These notes soon exceeded the story in length. A decade later, he had 50 pages of notes and diagrams for a 28-page short story.

The story of Kepler's *Dream* is set in a series of concentric frames. The outermost narrator is Kepler himself, who, after going out to watch the stars and the moon, falls into a deep sleep. He dreams he is reading a book, which begins "My name is Duracotus; my native land Iceland, which the ancients called Thule. My mother was Fiolxhilde . . ." (these lines alone have three footnotes covering a page and a half).

This second narrator's mother, Fiolxhilde, is a wise woman who gathers herbs, carries on mysterious rites, and sells magical wind charms to Icelandic sailors. After Duracotus ruins one of her charms by peeking inside, she sells

Joannis Keppleri
Somnium, five Astronomia Lunaris.

Um anno 1608. ferverent diffidia inter fratres Imp: Rudolphum et Matthiam Archidu- cem ; eorumque actiones vulgo ad exempla re- ferrent, ex historia Bohemica petita ; ego publi- ca vulgi curiositate excitus, ad Bohemica legenda animum appuli. Cumque incidissem in historiam Libussæ Viragi- nis, arte Magica celebratissimæ: factum quadam nocte, vt post contemplationem siderum et Lunæ, lecto composi- tus, altius obdormiscerem: atque mihi per somnum visus sum librum ex Nundinis allatum perlegere, cuius hic erat tenor:

Mihi[1] Duracoto nomen est, patria [2] Islandia, quam veteres Thulen dixère:[3] mater erat Fiolxhildis, quæ [4] nuper mortua, scri- bendi mihi peperit licentiam, cujus rei cupiditate pridē arsi.[5] Dum viveret, hoc diligenter egit, ne scriberem. Dicebat enim, multos esse perniciosos osores artium,[6] qui quod præ hebetudine mentis non capiunt, id calumnientur ;[7] legesq̄ figant injuriosas humano gene- ri;[8] quibus sanè legibus non pauci damnati,[9] Heclæ voraginibus fuerint absorpti.[10] Quod nomen esset patri meo, ipsa nunquam di- xit,[11] piscatorem fuisse, & centum quinquaginta annorum senem

A   *deces-*

---

him to a sea captain, who takes him to Tycho Brahe's island Hven, where he learns astronomy. After five years, he finds his way home. His remorseful mother is delighted by his return and his new knowledge of astronomy. What he has learned from books, she says, she was taught by a gentle and innocuous daemon. She agrees to summon the daemon to teach Duracotus about "Levania," as the moon is known by its inhabitants. They foregather at a crossroads, Fiolxhilde speaks some words, and after covering their heads with their coats, they hear the raspy, indistinct voice of the daemon.

The daemon, now the third narrator, tells about how the heavens appear viewed from the moon. The day-to-day phenomena are quite different, as Kepler knew. On the earth, a day is 24 hours long, during which time the moon goes around the sky once, while it takes a month to return to where it was among the stars, going from new moon to full moon to new moon again as it does so. On the moon, because one side always faces toward the earth, the earth just hangs in one place on the sky, "as though," Kepler writes, "it were affixed to the heavens with a nail." It revolves in 24 hours as it hangs there, for which reason Kepler's lunar inhabitants call it "Volva." Their day corresponds to a cycle of lunar phases, so it lasts a whole month.

Of course, if one face of the moon always faces the earth, the other hemisphere always faces away. For this reason, the near side of the moon is called "Subvolva" (under Volva) and the far side is called "Privolva" (deprived of Volva). Lacking the moderating influence Volva has on the long, hot days and the long, cold nights, Privolva is a wilderness roamed by hoards of scavenging nomads, while in Subvolva civilization has taken root.

Unfortunately, Kepler did not say much more about the alien creatures who inhabit the moon. His emphasis throughout is on astronomy and on astronomical appearances as viewed from the moon, and he does not exploit his set-up for any broader literary purpose. Almost as soon as he begins to stray into fanciful descriptions of creatures, he wakes up with his head covered by his pillow, a joke referring back to the ritual of summoning the demon in the dream.

It is not the story line of the *Somnium* but the literary genre that is of interest. Some say that Kepler's use of scientific knowledge to create a detailed framework for a fictional account of another world makes the *Somnium* an important early work of science fiction. The notes—although they are inserted so thickly that they make it nearly impossible to concentrate on the story—are more interesting in themselves, for they reveal some of Kepler's speculative insights.

For example, he describes quite clearly the point between the earth and the moon where the gravitational attractions of each body exactly cancel.

The printing of the *Somnium* was suspended when Kepler was able to help again with the ephemerides. But it was resumed when it became necessary for him to go on a business trip in October. His finances were in trouble again. First, he had 3,500 florins invested in Upper Austria. After a year of getting the runaround, he had been promised the payment of his interest if he presented himself on November 11 in Linz. Second, Wallenstein had been deposed as supreme general of the imperial army in August. Emperor Ferdinand II never called a meeting of the Imperial Diet, but he did need the support of the seven powerful electoral states, those states of the empire that had a vote in the election of a new emperor. At the meeting of the imperial electors in Regensburg in the summer of 1630, Ferdinand came under pressure from the electors, who feared Wallenstein's great power. They demanded Wallenstein's resignation, and Ferdinand complied. Since Kepler had become so dependent on Wallenstein, his patron's fall from grace was serious business, especially in the matter of the nearly 12,000 florins he was owed by the emperor. It would be strategic to visit the meeting of the electors in Regensburg and see for himself how things stood.

Kepler set off on October 8, 1630. In order to be ready for any eventuality, he took with him nearly every scrap of documentation concerning his wealth. In addition, he shipped a huge stock of books ahead to Leipzig, including 57 copies of the ephemerides for the years 1621–1636, which they had been printing furiously in order to finish. He also sent 16 copies of the *Rudolfine Tables* and 73 other assorted books. He would be stopping at the fall fair in Leipzig and wanted to have stock to sell. The stress of finishing the printing and the uncertainty of what faced him at court put him in a desperate frame of mind. As he rode out of town, his family thought it more likely to see the Day of Judgment than ever to see him alive again.

After the fair in Leipzig, he sent the wagoneer ahead to Regensburg and followed a few days later. On November 2, cold, tired, and saddle sore, he rode over the Stone Bridge into Regensburg on an old nag, which he sold upon his arrival for 11 florins. Traveling in the chilly autumn air had made him sick. At first, he shrugged it off as a nuisance, but then he grew worse. A high fever gripped him and he became delirious. A doctor was summoned, who bled him, but it did not help. Finally, men of God came to his bedside to console him.

He drifted in and out of consciousness for a few days, trying when he was lucid to express that he had done his best to bring the Protestants and the Catholics together. But the hateful Protestant pastor replied that that was like thinking that he could reconcile Christ with Satan. Finally, as he approached the end of his life, he was asked on what he pinned his hope for salvation. Kepler answered confidently, "Solely on the merit of our savior Jesus Christ, in which is founded all refuge, solace, and deliverance." He died at noon on November 15, 1630.

He was buried in the Protestant cemetery of St. Peter outside Regensburg's city wall two days later, after a funeral procession including some of the empire's most illustrious men, who had gathered in Regensburg for the meeting of the electors. Witnesses reported that, on that evening, fiery balls fell from heaven. We now recognize such meteors to be natural phenomena. In Kepler's time, however, when such displays were perceived as supernatural omens, it might have seemed that the heavens themselves were weeping for their interpreter.

The location of Johannes Kepler's final resting place is no longer known. The storms of the religious intolerance and war that buffeted his life did not let him rest peacefully even in death. Scarcely a few years later, Swedish forces besieged and captured Regensburg and then were expelled in turn by Bavarian and imperial troops. Whether by the city's defenders or attackers, the churchyard and Kepler's grave were eradicated in the process.

Our only record of Kepler's grave is a sketch of the gravestone made by a friend. It contained a description of his career as mathematician to three emperors, and proclaimed him foremost among astronomers. In addition, it carried an epitaph written by Kepler himself, which read:

> *I measured the heavens,*
> *Now the earth's shadows I measure,*
> *My mind was already in the heavens,*
> *Now the shadow of my body rests.*

The only record of Kepler's tombstone in Regensburg is this sketch by a friend.

Vindication

The sheer mathematical complexity of employing Kepler's laws of planetary motion and his unusual commitment to celestial physics ensured that the reception of his ideas would be problematic in the astronomical community of his time. In the end, it would be the tremendous increase in the accuracy of the prediction of planetary positions that would force astronomers to grapple with them. Only a handful of astronomers immediately recognized Kepler's accomplishment.

Toward the end of his life, Kepler foresaw a pair of upcoming celestial events that had never been witnessed before. His theory of Mercury predicted that Mercury would pass across the face of the sun on November 7, 1631. (Venus would likewise transit a month later, though it would not be visible in Europe.) The invention of the telescope and methods of using it to project an image of the sun onto a white screen had allowed astronomers to observe sunspots in the early 1610s. The same technology would allow them to observe Mercury in transit for the first time. Excited by this prospect, Kepler wanted to spread the news as widely as possible, so that observers throughout Europe could try to witness it. In 1629, he published an eight-page pamphlet entitled

De raris mirisque anni 1631 phaenomenis, Veneris puta Mercurii in Solem incursu, admonitio ad astronomos, rerumque coelestium studiosos (A Warning to Astronomers and Those Interested in Celestial Matters regarding the Rare and Amazing Phenomena of 1631, Namely, the Incursion of Venus and Mercury into the Sun) in which he predicted the phenomena and gave instructions for observing them. Alas, Kepler died before he could witness the extraordinary event he predicted.

Forewarned, astronomers set up telescopes to observe the transit of Mercury on November 7, 1631. Though Kepler's prediction was very slightly off, the transit occurred within 6 hours of the predicted time. "I have found him," exclaimed Pierre Gassendi in an open letter from France, "I have seen him where no one has ever seen him before!" Astronomers had to acknowledge that Kepler's planetary theory was at least 20 times more accurate than anyone else's.

Only toward the end of the 17th century, in the work of Isaac Newton, was the physical necessity of Kepler's three laws demonstrated. Newton succeeded in codifying the laws of mechanics and gravity and in using them to describe the dynamics of the solar system with unprecedented success. He showed how the motion of inertial bodies under the influence of gravity was necessarily described by Kepler's laws. Newtonian physics was entirely different in conception from Kepler's celestial physics, so it was inevitable that he dismissed Kepler's principles.

Though Kepler was never forgotten as an astronomer of genius and for a number of fundamental discoveries—the three important laws of planetary motion still bear his name—it was only when scholars began to focus their attention on the nature of scientific knowledge and the modes of thinking scientifically that Kepler's thought began to be examined in all its complexity. It can be said that it took the acquaintance with Albert Einstein's genius for scholars fully to appreciate his kindred intellect in Johannes Kepler.

December 27, 1571
Born in Weil der Stadt, Germany

1584–1588
Attends seminary school at Adelberg and Maulbronn

1589–1594
Attends the University of Tübingen, where he receives a
B.A. (by examination, 1588) and M.A. (1591); nearly com-
pletes three additional years of study in theology

April 1594
Arrives in Graz, Styria, to assume the position of mathematics teacher and district mathematician

1596–March 1597
Printing of the *Mysterium* cosmographicum in Tübingen

April 27, 1597
Marries Barbara Müller

September 28, 1598
Counter-Reformation begins in Styria; Protestant teachers
and preachers expelled from Graz; Kepler is allowed to
return after about a month

January-June 1600
Visits Tycho Brahe at Benatky Castle

September 30, 1600
Leaves Styria with his family and all their possessions
when all remaining Protestants are banished

October 24, 1601
Tycho Brahe dies; two days later, Kepler is named his suc-
cessor as imperial mathematician to Rudolf II in Prague

1604
Publishes the *Astronomia pars optica*

Around Easter, 1605
Discovers the elliptical form of Mars's orbit

1609
Astronomia nova finally published

March 1610
Galileo publishes the *Sidereus nuncius* containing his telescopic discoveries; Kepler responds, publishing the *Dissertatio cum nunceo sidereo* in Prague in May

Summer 1611
Kepler publishes *Dioptrice,* containing explanation of the
telescope

July 3, 1611
Barbara Kepler dies

January 20, 1612
Holy Roman Emperor Rudolf II dies; Archduke Matthias
succeeds him

May 1612
Begins work as mathematician to the Estates of Upper
Austria in Linz

October 30, 1613
Marries Susanna Reuttinger

July 1615
Publishes *Nova stereometria doliorum vinariorum* in Linz

Fall 1617
Publishes the first volume of *Epitome astronomiae Copernicanae* in Linz

Fall 1617–early 1618
Returns to Württemberg with his mother, but her court
case is delayed

May 15, 1618
Discovers his third law of planetary motion

May 23, 1618
"Defenestration of Prague"; Thirty Years War begins

1619

Harmonice mundi libri V published in Linz

March 20, 1619

Holy Roman Emperor Matthias dies; Archduke Ferdinand
II suceeds him 5 months later

Early 1620

Second volume of *Epitome astronomiae Copernicanae* published in Linz

August 7, 1620–August 1621

Katharina Kepler arrested for witchcraft; Johannes Kepler
returns to Württemberg to assist in her defense

Fall 1621

Final volume of the *Epitome astronomiae Copernicanae* published in Frankfurt

October 1625

Counter-Reformation begins in Upper Austria

November 1626

Kepler and his family leave Linz

December 1626-September 1627

Rudolfine Tables printed in Ulm

July 1628

Kepler arrives in Sagan to become personal mathematician to General Wallenstein; Counter-Reformation in
Sagan begins four months later

November 15, 1630

Dies while visiting a meeting of imperial electors in
Regensburg

Works by Kepler in English translation

Epitome of Copernican Astronomy, Bks. IV and V, & *Harmonies of the World*, Bk. V. Trans. Charles Glenn Wallis. 1952. Reprint, New York: Prometheus Books, 1995.

The Harmony of the World. Trans. E. J. Aiton, A. M. Duncan, and J. V. Field. Philadelphia: American Philosophical Society, 1997.

Kepler's Conversation with Galileo's Sidereal Messenger. Trans. Edward Rosen. New York: Johnson Reprint Corp., 1965.

Kepler's Somnium: The Dream or Posthumous Work on Lunar Astronomy. Trans. Edward Rosen. Madison: University of Wisconsin Press, 1967.

Mysterium cosmographicum: The Secret of the Universe. Trans. A. M. Duncan. New York: Abaris Books, 1981.

New Astronomy. Trans. William H. Donahue. Cambridge: Cambridge University Press, 1992.

The Six-Cornered Snowflake. Trans. Colin Hardie. Oxford: Clarendon Press, 1966.

Works about Kepler

Baumgartner, Carola. *Johannes Kepler: Life and Letters*. New York: Philosophical Library, 1951.

Caspar, Max. *Kepler*. Trans. C. Doris Hellman. Introduction and References by Owen Gingerich. Bibliographical Citations by Owen Gingerich and Alain Segonds. 1948. New York: Dover, 1993.

Field, J. V. *Kepler's Geometrical Cosmology*. Chicago: University of Chicago Press, 1988.

———. "A Lutheran Astrologer: Johannes Kepler." *Archive for History of Exact Sciences* 31 (1984): 189-272.

Gingerich, Owen. *The Eye of Heaven: Ptolemy, Copernicus, Kepler*. New York: American Institute of Physics, 1993.

———. "Kepler, Johannes." In *Dictionary of Scientific Biography,* ed. Charles Coulston Gillispie, vol. 7, pp. 289-312. New York: Scribners, 1973.

Holton, Gerald. "Kepler's Universe: Its Physics and Metaphysics." *American Journal of Physics* 24 (1956): 340-351. Reprinted in

Gerald Holton, *Thematic Origins of Scientific Thought: Kepler to Einstein*, 53-74. Revised ed., Cambridge: Harvard University Press, 1988.

Jardine, Nicholas. *The Birth of History and Philosophy of Science: Kepler's* A Defence of Tycho against Ursus *with Essays on Its Provenance and Significance*. Cambridge: Cambridge University Press, 1984.

Koestler, Arthur. *The Sleepwalkers: A History of Man's Changing Vision of the Universe*. New York: Macmillan, 1959.

Koyré, Alexandre. *The Astronomical Revolution: Copernicus—Kepler—Borelli*. Trans. R. E. W. Maddison. 1973. Reprint, New York: Dover, 1992.

Kozamthadam, Job. *The Discovery of Kepler's Laws: The Interaction of Science, Philosophy, and Religion*. Notre Dame, Ind.: University of Notre Dame Press, 1994.

Rosen, Edward. *Three Imperial Mathematicians: Kepler Trapped between Tycho Brahe and Ursus*. New York: Abaris Books, 1986.

Stephenson, Bruce. *Kepler's Physical Astronomy*. 1987. Reprint, Princeton: Princeton University Press, 1994.

———. *The Music of the Spheres: Kepler's Harmonic Astronomy*. Princeton: Princeton University Press, 1994.

Wilson, Curtis. "How Did Kepler Discover His First Two Laws?" *Scientific American* 236 (1972): 92-106.

Related Reading

Hoskin, Michael, ed. *The Cambridge Illustrated History of Astronomy*. Cambridge: Cambridge University Press, 1997.

Thoren, Victor E. *The Lord of Uraniborg: A Biography of Tycho Brahe*. Cambridge: Cambridge University Press, 1990.

Taton, René, and Curtis Wilson, eds. *Planetary Astronomy from the Renaissance to the Rise of Astrophysics, Part A: Tycho Brahe to Newton*. Cambridge: Cambridge University Press, 1989.

Westfall, Richard S. *The Construction of Modern Science: Mechanisms and Mechanics*. Cambridge: Cambridge University Press, 1977.

AUTHORS

James R. Voelkel is an historian of science whose research has centered on Johannes Kepler and Tycho Brahe. He is a graduate of Williams College, Cambridge University, and Indiana University, where he received a Ph.D. in History of Science. He is currently Capabilities Manager of the History of Recent Science and Technology web project located at the Dibner Institute for the History of Science and Technology in Cambridge, Massachusetts. He has taught astronomy and history of science at Williams College, Harvard University, and the Johns Hopkins University.

Owen Gingerich is a senior astronomer at the Smithsonian Astrophysical Observatory and Professor of Astronomy and of the History of Science at Harvard University. He has served as vice president of the American Philosophical Society and as chairman of the U.S. National Committee of the International Astronomical Union. The author of more than 400 articles and reviews, Professor Gingerich is also the author of *The Great Copernicus Chase and Other Adventures in Astronomical History* and *The Eye of Heaven: Ptolemy, Copernicus, Kepler.* The International Astronomical Union's Minor Planet Bureau has named Asteroid 2658 "Gingerich" in his honor.